Let Me
Learn

To my children, Joel, Joy, and Jane;
to my grandchildren, Emily Joy and Noah Thomas;
and
to your children, with love

Let Me Learn

Christine A. Johnston

CORWIN PRESS, INC.
A Sage Publications Company
Thousand Oaks, California

For information:

Corwin Press, Inc.
A Sage Publications Company
2455 Teller Road
Thousand Oaks, California 91320
E-mail: order@corwinpress.com

SAGE Publications Ltd.
6 Bonhill Street
London EC2A 4PU
United Kingdom

SAGE Publications India Pvt. Ltd.
M-32 Market
Greater Kailash I
New Delhi 110 048 India

Printed in the United States of America

Library of Congress Cataloging-in-Publication Data

Johnston, Christine A.
    Let me learn / Christine A. Johnston.
        p. cm.
    Includes bibliographical references and index.

    ISBN 0-8039-6764-0 (cloth: acid-free paper)
    ISBN 0-8039-6765-9 (pbk.: acid-free paper)
    1. Learning, Psychology of. 2. Learning, Psychology of—Case studies.   I. Title.
    LB1060.J475 1998
    370.15′23—ddc21   98-19722

This book is printed on acid-free paper.

98 99 00 01 02 03 04 10 9 8 7 6 5 4 3 2 1

Production Editor: S. Marlene Head
Editorial Assistant: Julia Parnell
Typesetter: Rebecca Evans
Cover Designer: Michelle Lee

Contents

We are surrounded by talk of learning styles, brain science, and multiple intelligences. Can any of these make a difference for the learner? The opening chapters of Let Me Learn explain that there is more to learning than style, neuroscience, and multiple intelligences. What is vital to successful learning is hearing and listening to the voice of the learner.

Chapter 1 introduces the voice of the learner and suggests what research has identified as the consequences of not recognizing and addressing the learner's call for help.

Chapter 2 identifies the source of the voice of the learner and presents a cogent explanation of the learning process.

Chapter 3 explains how to capture definitively the voice and message of the learner.

Chapter 4 details the pain, frustration, and challenge of listening for the voice of the learner you just can't reach.

Foreword

The reader might well ask why the Ambassador of Malta agreed to write the foreword to a book on learning. I have chosen to share my views on learning because I am very aware of how we frequently fail to see that for many children (too many children), just entering a classroom is a real ordeal. I have chosen to write the foreword to this particular book because I believe that the Let Me Learn Process is the best way to address our orthodox educational system, which can be most unforgiving! In contrast to the monolithic educational system, which enslaves the student, Let Me Learn frees the student to be a learner who uses his or her learning cleverness. The freeing of the learner begins when the teacher and learner form a learning partnership. In such a partnership, the teacher unfetters the learner within the child, allowing, as Michelangelo said, "the image that is already there" to emerge.

What this text on learning vividly describes is the power that is released when students possess knowledge about their learning and are freed to use it within their classrooms. In my case, it was my mother's friend, Auntie Anna Salomone, who served as a brilliant source of inspiration and, most of all, courage to me as a learner. Without this partnership, the story that follows would have had a very different ending.

To this day, I can remember how, as a little boy, I dreaded school! The day was very long. It began with the ordeal of getting on the bus and being driven through forbidding gates toward an austere building. I hated the smell of the school's pristine cleanliness. Upon arrival, we were regimented from one line into another with military precision and then seated in a dismal classroom. The story of my learning stops there.

We were given piles and piles of books and an immense amount of homework. My powers of concentration were seriously lacking, and it was difficult for me to stay on track. One word, one beautiful sentence got me off to another world. And so it was always with a flutter of great happiness and anticipation that I got back on the bus that would take me home—until the following day, when the same ordeal began again.

Fortunately for me, my mother and her dear friend, Auntie Anna, joined forces to form a great partnership that freed and enabled my learning. Working under their tutelage, I found myself in a system of learning that had at its heart the very essence of the Let Me Learn Process. Their dedication was primarily to the learner. That was vital for my survival as a learner because I was not the epitome of the student whose diligence showed in neat handwriting and attention to duty. First of all, I was not a willing memorizer of material I found uninteresting. Oh, to be certain, I *could* memorize. It simply was not the manner in which learning appealed to me. My classmates who had the propensity and disposition to absorb the information being propounded were labeled extremely bright because they could memorize and concentrate, but what some of them were doing was parroting what they studied, and what they knew did not always translate well outside of school, where they were expected to make decisions.

Yale's eminent cognitive psychologist, Robert Sternberg, made this same point when he expressed profound disappointment at the quality of students arriving at his university, boasting high IQs and excellent performance on examinations but deficient in what is called the "practical" and "creative" intelligences. His concern was that these learners, born with incredible powers of imagination and capacity for problem solving, had progressively learned not to think, not to apply problem solving to real-life situations. "People with 'successful intelligence,'" says Sternberg, "recognize and play to their strengths while recognizing and trying to compensate for their limitations." The Let Me Learn Process does just that!

Thus, I have chosen to champion the Let Me Learn Process because I have experienced the effect of a teacher-learner partnership that is based on freeing the learner to use his or her learning processes to the utmost potential. My belief in the message and process of *Let Me Learn*, however, does not rest solely with my experience as a learner.

I am a believer in *Let Me Learn* because it is an empirically tested approach that dedicates itself solely to unlocking the different abilities of the learners, helping them find the path for learning that is best for them. I describe the process as a compass pointing to the empty horizon, which takes as its first bearing the individual needs of the learner. I have personally witnessed the positive results that the Let Me Learn Process has on children whose voices are heard and whose message helps establish productive learning partnerships. I have visited schools and spoken with students and teachers alike and have been incredibly impressed with how this process brings out the various kinds of learning that exist within the child and unlocks those threads that were not strong elements so that each individual is given the opportunity to flourish. I have seen the relief in the eyes of children who otherwise would be lost to an unrelenting, unforgiving system.

I am also a believer because the Let Me Learn Process has universal appeal and application. In fact, the process has evolved on the basis of children's voices from around the world being heard and responded to by those who have researched, tested, and developed this approach within their national boundaries. Within the pages of this book, the reader will find numerous examples of children from all over the globe who have been involved in the Let Me Learn Process and have experienced its empowering effects.

I am a believer in the Let Me Learn Process because it speaks to teachers, the guardians of our children's learning. This important book helps teachers distinguish between the lesson and the learner, giving primary focus to the needs of the latter. Too frequently, a teacher comes to the classroom with a well-prepared lesson, but the children do not learn as the teacher intended. Perhaps the learner is disinterested in the scope of the lesson or feels that the particular lesson is futile or irrelevant to him or her.

The message of *Let Me Learn* explains how differences experienced in the classroom between the learner and the lesson are frequently due to the learner's inability to see the lesson's relevance, significance, or value. Our reaction to such students is to criticize, label, and then write them off as not conforming to the norm of our instruction. This is not a new phenomenon. St. Thomas Aquinas, for example, was referred to by his teachers as a dumb ox!

This unfortunate attitude has been prevalent since ancient Greece, when complex forms of human thought were given the form of the epic lesson. Some learners listened in awe and disbelief at the magnificence of the lesson. However, it was those learners who did not understand the epic lesson who were the real victims of what society at that time viewed as the standardized, acceptable, high-achieving way to learn. Even today, conventional methods of learning leave out in the cold those minds whose brilliance does not appear through rote memorization, standardized tests, or paper-and-pencil exercises. Because the teacher is not an all-knowing individual and is also a product of his or her environment, an objective method to identify the needs of the learner, such as the Learning Combination Inventory explained at length in this text, is an indispensable element in the classroom.

I am a believer in the message of *Let Me Learn*. Its message resonates with my experience as a learner; its message is one that I have seen in the voices and actions of learners within classrooms; its message can be universally applied; and its process frees teachers to let their children learn!

As suggested at the beginning of the foreword, the story of my evolving as a learner would likely have ended quite differently were it not for those teachers whose sculpting freed me to use my own unique learning processes. Thus, if I am allowed some leniency with this foreword, I would like to dedicate my closing remarks to my teachers—past, present, and future.

My most recent teacher and friend has been my Minister of Foreign Affairs, who has taught me the fundamental lesson of the good diplomat: The bearer of the message must carry the truth faithfully. The ability of the ambassador, who is a mere messenger, is to teach himself or herself when and how to employ that message so that the truth becomes the fire that can "pull and stretch the metal" required to build bridges between nations great and small.

Most of all, I wish to thank my friend and teacher, Dr. Christine Johnston, for her efforts to bring before us not just the plight of learners but a process of hope that lets each child learn. Her words have explained to me how a restless, curious young boy, that same young boy described at the beginning of the foreword, could teach himself to learn whatever was required of him. Therefore, it is with deepest admiration for the powerful message of *Let Me Learn* that I conclude this foreword.

DR. MARK ANTHONY MICALLEF
Ambassador of Malta
March 1998
Washington, DC

Preface

Let Me Learn is about listening to the learner. It is not a book about curriculum, or grouping, or assessment, although all of these issues are addressed. The sole purpose of Let Me Learn is to help educators create a listening environment in which they can hear the voice of the learner, understand the learner, and facilitate the learner's success. Within the pages of this text, the reader will hear the voices of teachers and the stories of the children they pulled back from the brink of frustration. These are the stories of success in the classroom—success because the teacher listened to the quiet voice of the learner—the inner voice that asks for only one thing: "Let me learn."

The Features

Let Me Learn has several unique features. First, each chapter begins with its own flyleaf. The flyleaf consists of a provocative thought or question intended to focus the reader upon the issues addressed in the chapter that follows. Second, the book uses many authoring voices. There is the researcher-academic-practitioner, the elementary learning consultant, the secondary school teacher, the curriculum specialist, and the school administrator. These are the voices of experience! Even more importantly, these are the voices of elementary, middle school, high school, and adult learners explaining how learning works best for them. There is much that can be learned from these voices. A third unique feature is "And this is what they said," a quotation found in the chapter just read that is intended to provoke discussion or further thought. A list of suggested readings is provided at the end of the book.

The Overview

Part I

Part I (Chapters 1-5) focuses on the importance of listening to the voices of learners as they explain how learning works for them. Chapter 1 introduces the voice of the learner and suggests the consequences for both learner and teacher if the learner's voice is ignored. Chapter 2 explains the source of the learner's voice. Chapter 3 describes how to capture the voice of the learner through the use of the Learning Combination Inventory (LCI), an internationally validated learning instrument. Within this chapter, the reader has an opportunity to complete the LCI and interpret its results.

Chapter 4 reveals the most underrated and least understood voice among all the learners within the classroom. If a reader were allowed to read only one chapter in this text, Chapter 4 is the "must read" chapter. In it are vivid examples of the "un" student—uninterested, unmotivated, unengaged, and unreachable. However, the chapter does not leave the reader in a state of bewilderment or frustration. It explains how to listen to the voice of these learners and engage them in meaningful and relevant learning. This chapter is the heart and conscience of the text.

Chapter 5 forms a bridge between Part I and Part II of the book by moving the reader beyond awareness to action. Within this chapter, the reader learns how to develop teacher-learner partnerships that link the needs of the learner to the realities of the classroom. It includes the presentation of two codes: the Code for Responsible Learning and the Code for Responsible Teaching. Both codes reiterate the central message of the text: *Let Me Learn* is about listening and responding to the voice of the learner.

Part II

Part II consists of four chapters, each featuring the experiences of various educators who took seriously the voice of the learner. Each developed effective professional behaviors in response to the message, "Let me learn!" The four chapters that compose Part II tell the firsthand experiences of what the Let Me Learn Process looks and sounds like when implemented within *real* classrooms and *real* school settings. This is the exemplar section of the text. It includes learning activities used by teachers of elementary, middle, and secondary school students who have engaged successfully in the Let Me Learn Process.

Chapter 6 begins this section with the stories of elementary teachers who used the Let Me Learn Process within their classrooms and learned to respond effectively to the voices of their students. Chapter 7 tells of the challenge of implementing the Let Me Learn Process in the secondary school. It includes examples of teachers who changed their focus from subject matter only to include listening to the voice of their learners.

Chapter 8 is a chapter that provides a reality check for the reader. In this chapter, the reader hears the voices of six teachers as they engaged in a Let Me Learn staff development program. The pathway to change and growth was neither direct nor easy. However, the focus of the learner's voice provided the reason to persist in the process, a process that led to important insights into themselves as teachers and into their students as learners.

Chapter 9 concludes Part II and is the story of a school administrator who let the voices of students, teachers, and parents guide her in the development of leadership behaviors that were attuned to the learner. This chapter gives hope to those teachers and administrators who feel mired in the top-down, fad-of-the-moment approach to staff development. Here is a refreshing approach to how a leader can facilitate change for the purpose of serving the learner.

Part III

Part III moves the reader from the stories of teachers and administrators, who found success by listening to the learner's voice, to the broader implications of using the Let Me Learn Process. Chapter 10 concludes with the same laser-beam focus with which the book began: the learner's voice. The learner's voice is what teaching, learning, and education are all about. Once we understand this, we can move forward and address the gnawing, perennial "Yes . . . , buts" of standardized tests, state-mandated curricula, and parents' expectations. The message of *Let Me Learn* would not be complete without confronting these issues and providing a reasonable means of addressing them. After all, none of the message of the previous nine chapters matters if, after all is *read* and done, nothing is put in place for the learners with whom the reader comes into contact!

If we are committed to making a difference with learners, we will do so by listening to their voices and supporting their successful learning behaviors. When that is achieved, *Let Me Learn* moves from being the voice of the solo learner to a chorus of classmates and teachers who join in saying, "Let us learn, together, successfully!"

About the Author

Christine A. Johnston is Associate Professor of Educational Administration at Rowan College of New Jersey. She earned an EdD in administration and supervision from Rutgers University, an MA in urban planning from the University of Wisconsin–Milwaukee, and a BA in secondary education from the University of Wisconsin–Eau Claire. Her career has been shaped by opportunities provided through a Ford Foundation Internship, a National Science Foundation Fellowship, and a New Jersey Governor's Teacher's Grant. Her professional life has spanned three decades of teaching, administration, collaboration, and research in public schools and government agencies. She has been especially successful in building local, national, and international partnerships that bridge the gap from conceptualization to practical application. A dedicated researcher and enthusiastic presenter, she has focused her concern on the nurturing of real schools, real students, and real educators through attention to effective communication, a clear understanding of the learning process, and a commitment to the student-centered classroom. She is the author of *Empowering the Organization Through Professional Talk* (1994) and *Unlocking the Will to Learn* (Corwin Press, 1996).

*And after the fire there was
the soft whisper of a voice.*

1 Kings 19.12

Part 1

Getting in the Mind-Set to Listen to the Learner

We are surrounded by talk of learning styles, brain science, and multiple intelligences. Can any of these make a difference for the learner? The opening chapters of Let Me Learn *explain that there is more to learning than style, neuroscience, and multiple intelligences. What is vital to successful learning is hearing and listening to the voice of the learner.*

---

*Learners must find their own voice
rather than have experts speaking "at them"
or "for them" or "about them."*

Lynch and O'Neil, 1994, p. 315

Who Is Prepared to Answer the Learner's Call?

The power of thought and the spoken word. The inside-out of our kids. All we have to do is listen to them. They will guide us if we can get beyond their space and heart and anger. They will tell us who they are and, if we listen, they will guide our learning together—whether we use structure or details or tools or ideas, we are of value. We have a reason to be and so much to contribute. Listen, listen, listen—listen to the pain, listen for the potential. What a challenge we have—what an opportunity what a responsibility—we can do it if we use all of who and what we are.

C. Johnston (1996)
Evesham Township
Inclusion Workshop Journal

The Sounds of Learning

Within our classrooms today, the 19th-century maxims of "Silence is golden," "Speak when you are spoken to," and "Children should be seen and not heard" are very much with us. Robert Sylwester presses the ridiculousness of this when he asks, "What is the difference between a human being and a tree? Answer: The ability to move and to communicate. Why then do we tell children to sit down and quit talking?"

Why do our schools continue to function with the unspoken message that when in a classroom, "It is better for children to be seen and not heard . . . until I call on them"? The answer is simple. With 20 or more students in a room, teaching requires good management. It requires time for teacher talk and time for student responses. It requires rules to regulate the stop-and-go of talk, the ebb and flow of conversation. Classroom management is an effort to prevent chaos and to provide an environment in which learning can occur. The irony is that every time we strive for a quiet learning environment, we are quelling the sound of learning and the voice of the learner who is seeking to clarify a direction, ask a key question, find an opportunity to talk one-on-one, or declare a "light bulb" experience. Much of this talk, the talk of the Let Me Learn voice within the child, gets lost in the talk of management, controlled communication, and unanswered calls for help.

A Call for Help

Noise? Sounds? Or communication? Which is it? If we maintain that the classroom needs to be quiet enough to hear the proverbial pin drop, what happens to the voice of the learner who needs to communicate in order to learn? Amid the din of a classroom that is frequently too small to accommodate all of the activity of learning, how can the learner's voice be heard? The challenge for the teacher is to hear the learner's call for help within any given classroom context. Without the teacher's awareness, how can the learner let the teacher know that there is an emergency? An idea is suffocating? An assignment is stranded on the top floor with no means of finding its way to safe completion. The only route to achieving the teacher's expectations is inaccessible. The atmosphere in the classroom is so filled with confusion that the learner can't see a way through it. How can the learner communicate this to the teacher?

Frequently within our classrooms, the urgent call of the learner goes unanswered because it is heard as a "prank" call, a call of inconvenience, or an interruption to the lesson. This breakdown in communication is most often the product of an educational system that holds the belief that teachers are to do the telling and teaching and children are to do the listening and learning. From what we know about the learning process, brain science, and the act of communication, it is clear that learning is an interactive and intra-active experience. Not only does the learner interact with those around him or her as the learning occurs, but the learner also interacts within himself or herself.

Two types of communication are occurring at the very least. One is the familiar interpersonal communication between the teacher and student that revolves around what is being taught. The other type of communication is intrapersonal. This is the communication within the learner asking, "Where have I heard this before? What do I already know about this that I can use? How did I respond to this idea, topic, activity before? What did I do that worked? What gave me a sense of success? Did I succeed? What did I learn that I have used successfully again and again? What have I learned outside of the classroom that helps me make sense of this new learning? What would make this more understandable? More interesting? Why do I want to know this?"

If the student were to communicate these messages out loud each time he or she is learning, we would say, "Please be quiet. Take your seat and listen." Actually, this is what occurs in the classroom when the internal communication of the learner is expressed externally. We don't understand that what we are hearing in the classroom is the expression of the learner's internal communication. Eventually, the learner stops communicating the important messages that would help all concerned with facilitating learning. The voice of the learner becomes muted amid teacher directions, limited time, and limited contact with others. Lost are the opportunities to clarify, probe, or communicate where the breakdown in understanding is occurring.

The Dilemma of Learner Versus Student

Why does the breakdown in communication and listening occur? Perhaps more to the point, why does the listening to the learner not take hold at the very beginning? The answer is simply that we do not believe that the child has anything to tell us about learning. Instead, we believe that we hold the key to unlocking the child's learning. We are convinced that the key to learning lies in converting the young learner into a successful student. Therefore, the child who enters school to learn enters a system that is intent upon turning him or her into a student.

The Difference Between a Student and a Learner: The 3 Rs

As a student of logic, I struggled with syllogisms, but I believe that stating the difference between a student and a learner in this manner makes the clearest case:

> A successful student may be a competent learner,
> but a competent learner is not always a successful student.

Competent learners are children who, at a rate appropriate to them, develop the intellectual, emotional, social, and problem-solving skills that allow them to function and contribute to the world around them. Competent students, on the other hand, are those children who accept the rules of school, absorb information at the rate of school, and perform the results of school in a manner that yields a passing cut-score on standardized student assessments.

Clearly, schooling can have a different effect upon a student and a learner. If we study the difference, we recognize that schooling involves formally training a person on how to conduct him- or herself in the place

Exhibit 1.1

called school. Learning, on the other hand, is a highly personal process by which the learner develops the ability to function in the world using his or her unique personalized abilities for doing so. Because learning begins long before schooling, entrance into school and its demands to alter how the child learns can be very stressful for both the learner and the teacher.

Recently, a first-grade teacher asked her students to draw a picture of where they do their learning. She was surprised to find that well over half of the students drew pictures of places other than school. Since hearing of that experience, I have encouraged other elementary teachers to have their students complete a similar assignment. The outcome has been the same.

Are You Listening Now?

It is very important for us to understand that children learn apart from school. In fact, when children first enter school, they have already spent the first 5 years of their lives using their natural learning patterns. We receive these experienced learners into our schools, and then we attempt to form them into students who can function in the school setting successfully. The difference between learners and students lies in the school's emphasis on what is deemed the acceptable learning process.

Exhibit 1.2

In fact, every time we, as teachers, say to our students, "Do the assignment in this manner," we are really saying, "Learn the way I am telling you to learn." Authentically teaching children to learn begins by identifying how learning works for individuals and then nurturing that awareness into a self-sufficient and successful learner. Some children will choose to listen and follow directions, write in workbooks, and practice their multiplication tables because that is truly how they learn. They are the first to experience success because their learning processes match the standard schooling processes.

Others will learn by trial and error, muddling through, and figuring things out. These learners run a much higher risk of being retained or classified at some point in their school experience, not because of a lack of aptitude but because the manner in which they learn does not fit the mold or criteria of a successful student.

Okay, You've Got My Attention

The literature on brain development tells us that by the time children enter school, they have already established their learning patterns. For example, at a recent White House conference on brain science and early

TABLE 1.1 What We Know About the Learner

The Age	The Stage	The Action	If Not Successful as a Student, the Question Becomes . . .
4-5	Induction	Enters school; seeks approval	Why am I able to learn at home and not at school?
6-8	Socialization	Develops standard behaviors through socialization in school setting	Why can't I learn the way the teacher wants me to learn?
9-10	Standardization	Develops awareness of self and teacher expectations	Why am I stupid in school?
11-12	Critical juncture	Decides to buy into schooling, or drops out as a learner	What does it matter if I'm stupid?

child development, experts in brain science explained that brain functions are based upon the wiring of the brain from the time of conception. It begins with the initial laying down of the circuitry and the running of test patterns before the connections are all made. Based upon the response it receives, the brain selects which pathways to keep and which to eliminate. In this way, the brain "grows." The brain is constantly testing how to focus and concentrate, recognize patterns, study the unfamiliar, and communicate. These developed patterns are what a child uses when he or she enters school. The research is clear—learning begins at conception, and the patterns of learning processes have begun to form long before formal schooling begins (see Table 1.1).

Reviewing the Pilgrimage of Learning

If we accept that learning begins long before formal schooling, and if we accept that the process by which individuals learn is well established before they enter the schoolyard gate, then we, as educators, are confronted with the dilemma of how best to determine the child's learning processes and help the child develop those processes in an effective and self-fulfilling manner.

At issue are two agendas: the teacher's agenda to school the child and develop a student, and the child's agenda to thrive in the school environment and learn about the world around him or her. The child can easily become confused by the expectation of the first and the desires of the second. This scenario is played out over and over again, classroom after classroom.

The mixed agendas of student versus learner are what contribute to the child's feeling that "I am not capable." I am not capable of doing my work. I am not capable of demonstrating my knowledge. I am not capable of doing my work in a way that is acceptable to my teacher. As a result of this conflict, the child is confused and begins to struggle with the question: To please the teacher, or not to please the teacher? To give in to the demands of being a good student (which the child is now beginning to think are the same as learning), or to stand alone against a finely tuned schooling machine? To admit that "I am not capable of being a learner in this school environment," or to rebel and ignore the threats of teachers and parents alike? The frustration and trauma resulting from making this choice are very real. With either choice, the child's self-esteem is seriously damaged. That damage can last a lifetime.

When the learner attempts to please the teacher and fit into the mold of a school-defined student, the learner begins to operate with great deliberateness and under much stress. The sense of what is not pleasing quickly shifts from "My schoolwork is not pleasing" to "I am not pleasing to the teacher." Now the child must decide to shift from developing skills as a learner to developing the skills of pleasing the teacher. It does not take much prompting for children to sense that they need to demonstrate knowledge or work in a manner different from the way they learn most naturally. For a young learner, it is very painful to come to the recognition that "the way in which I am doing my schoolwork or the way in which I think about things is not what the teacher expects, respects, or values."

To adapt one's natural process of learning is very difficult. As a result, many simply choose to opt out of the school program. Physically, they remain, but mentally, they abandon their interest or drive to succeed. This occurs as early as the third grade and is more than a U.S. phenomenon. Other nations have recognized the third year in school as being a pivotal point in the learner's development. For example, a report published by the Ministry of Education of Malta raises the question as to why there are so many referrals to child study teams at or around the third year of students' entrance into school. Australia has observed the same trend.

It appears that within 3 years of entry into school, the issue of learner versus student comes to a head. The teacher observes the learner's behavior and responds with, "You're falling behind. You're holding us back. You aren't developing at the same speed that I need to have you develop. You aren't performing at the same rate as you are supposed to. I have school achievement standards to meet. How am I going to address this? I have 22 other students. At least 11 of the 22 are moving along at an acceptable rate. They are responding to the learning process as it is being presented in this classroom. What's happening here? It can't be my teaching. I'm certain it can't be me because the other 11 are doing so well. It must be you."

And the child interprets the underlying message to be, "There is something wrong with me. I'm failing," and responds with, "I'm trying as hard as I can." All of this creates an emotional turmoil that causes the learner to feel unsuccessful and to question the purpose of schooling. The teacher also loses the sense of achievement. "I'm not getting through. What could I be doing differently? Why wasn't I taught what I need to know to help this child?" The frustration for both learner and teacher mounts. The teacher sees the learner as a "problem" student in the classroom: withdrawn, uncooperative, unresponsive to instruction, difficult, not performing up to grade-level standards. Unless resolved, what follows quite naturally are the standard actions of the schooling process: referral, testing, classifying, and labeling. This is an unhealthy experience for both the learner and the teacher.

How did it begin? It began when the teacher failed to hear the voice of the learner; it continued when the teacher sought to control and mute the voice of the learner. At this point, both the teacher and the learner began losing sight of the relationship between the learner and the learning process. There is a breakdown of communication. It continues as schooling replaces learning as the purpose for the child's presence in school.

What's a Teacher to Do?

First, the teacher needs to recognize that each learner has a unique set of learning processes that is revealed through his or her learning voice. Learners seek to have their voices heard. If they are heard, then a dialogue can begin. If they are ignored, then difficulty arises and the voice becomes a plea; a cry; an angry expression; unacceptable behavior; and, finally, silence.

This book is about learning how to listen above the din of standard classroom procedures to hear the distinct voice of the learner (see Table 1.2). Each of the ensuing chapters is intended to sharpen the reader's hearing, make each a better listener, and hone each into a more articulate facilitator of learning.

Achieving the skills to listen to the learner begins with the teacher developing an awareness of how he or she learns. This awareness evolves into an understanding of how an individual's learning processes become the individual's teaching behaviors. Finally, the awareness, when acted

TABLE 1.2 Teacher Goals When Using the Let Me Learn Process

Grades K-2: Provide an *accepting* environment.

1. Create teacher and parent awareness of the learner's voice.
2. Create learner acceptance of self as a capable learner.
3. Create teacher-learner communication.

Grades 3-5: Provide a *nurturing* environment in which the learner's patterned learning processes are developed.

1. Create peer awareness of unique learning processes.
2. Develop opportunities to work with other learners in a respectful learning environment.
3. Create teacher-learner partnerships.

Grades 6-8: Provide a *supportive* environment in which the learner begins to develop strategies to use the learning processes the learner would naturally avoid.

1. Create opportunities to move from a dependent/interdependent learning environment to an interdependent/independent one.
2. Create teacher-learner "okay times to talk" away from the limelight of peers.

Grades 9-12: Provide a *challenging* environment in which the learner exerts independence and resourcefulness in negotiating learning experiences.

1. Create opportunities for the learner to mature in learning behaviors while exercising choices for demonstrating knowledge and developing adaptation and growth strategies when required to operate using patterns that the learner would otherwise avoid.
2. Create teacher-learner mentorships.

upon, results in the development of a more effective classroom learning environment.

Getting Started on Learning How to Listen

The pages that follow provide a mind-bending read. They challenge each reader's mind-set on learning. Most importantly, this text equips the reader to make a difference with each learner, all year, one learner at a time!

And This Is What They Said

Competent learners are children who, at a rate appropriate to them, de-velop the intellectual, emotional, social, and problem-solving skills that allow them to function and contribute to the world around them. A stu-dent is someone who accepts the *rules* of school, absorbs information at the *rate* of school, and performs the *results* of school in a manner that yields a passing cut-score on standardized student assessments.

References and Selected Bibliography

Attard, P. (1995). *Government report.* Valetta, Malta: Ministry of Education.

Birrell, H. (1979). Stott's guide to the child's learning skills: A study in in-fant schools in Coventry. *A.E.P. Journal, 5,* 30-34.

Birrell, H., Phillips, C. J., & Stott, D. (1985). Learning style and school at-tainment in young children: A follow-up study. *School Psychology International, 6,* 207-218.

Borkowski, J., & Krause, A. (1985). Metacognition and attributional be-liefs. In G. d'Ydewalle (Ed.), *Cognition, information processing, and motivation* (pp. 557-567). Amsterdam: North-Holland/Elsevier.

Cohen, D. (1997, April 17). *Address.* Transcription of White House Confer-ence on Early Childhood Development and Learning, Washington, DC.

Cronbach, L. J., & Furby, L. (1970). How should we measure "change"—or should we? *Psychological Bulletin, 7,* 68-80.

Dweck, C. (1986). Motivational processes affecting learning. *American Psychologist, 41,* 1040-1048.

Eisner, E. (1997). Cognition and representation: A way to pursue the American dream? *Phi Delta Kappan, 78*(5), 349-360.

Green, L., Francis, J., & Stott, D. (1984). Confirmation of the relationship between children's learning styles and attainments by examination of discordant cases. *Human Learning, 3,* 295-304.

Hart, S., Leal, L., Burney, L., & Santulli, K. (1985). *Memory in the elemen-tary classroom: How teachers encourage strategy use.* Paper presented at the Society for Research in Child Development, Toronto, Canada.

Hill, D. (1991). Tasting failure: Thoughts of an at-risk learner. *Phi Delta Kappan, 73*(4), 308-310.

Johnston, C. (1996). *Unlocking the will to learn.* Thousand Oaks, CA: Corwin.

Johnston, C. (1997b). *Many voices—one message: A cross-cultural study of student learning processes with implications for learners, teachers, and reformers.* Paper presented at the European Institute on Research on Learning and Instruction Symposium, Athens, Greece.

Johnston, C., & Dainton, G. (1996). *The learning combination inventory.* Pittsgrove, NJ: Let Me Learn.

Kuhl, P. (1997, April 17). *Address.* Transcription of White House Conference on Early Childhood Development and Learning, Washington, DC.

Kurtz, B., & Borkowski, J. (1987). Development of strategic skills in impulsive and reflective children: A longitudinal study of metacognition. *Journal of Experimental Child Psychology, 23,* 129-148.

Lynch, K. & O'Neill, C. (1994). The colonisation of social class in education. *British Journal of Sociology of Education, 15*(3), 315.

Phillips, C. J., Stott, D., & Birrell, H. (1987). The effects of learning style on progress towards literacy and numeracy. *Educational Review, 39*(1), 31-40.

Pressley, M., Borkowski, J., & O'Sullivan, J. (1985). Metamemory and the teaching of strategies. In D. L. Forrest-Pressley, G. MacKinnon, & T. Waller (Eds.), *Metacognition, cognition, and human performance* (pp. 111-153). Orlando, FL: Academic Press.

Shatz, C. (1997, April 17). *Address.* Transcription of White House Conference on Early Childhood Development and Learning, Washington, DC.

Stott, D., Green, L., & Francis, J. (1983). Learning style and school attainment. *Human Learning, 2,* 61-75.

Sylwester, R. (1995). *A celebration of neurons: An educator's guide to the human brain.* Arlington, VA: Association for Supervision and Curriculum Development.

Sylwester, R. (1997). *Keynote address.* Presentation at the Seventh International Congress on Thinking, Singapore.

Weiner, B. (1979). A theory of motivation for some classroom experiences. *Journal of Educational Psychology, 71,* 3-25.

Further Reading

Elkind, D. (1981). *The hurried child: Growing up too fast, too soon.* Reading, MA: Addison-Wesley.

*There is nothing more liberating and supporting
for students who believe they will never be as smart
as the other kids, than to know how they learn and
be given permission to learn in those ways!*

Sandra Lazar
Personal journal, July 2, 1997
Rowan University

2

Who Is the "Me" in Let Me Learn?

Discovering the "Me" in Let Me Learn

Misidentification—something as simple as calling a student by the wrong name—can frustrate the learner. Recently, I heard resentment in the voice of a 13-year-old boy whose teacher repeatedly called him Danny. "It's Josh!" the young man said to me. "I'm Josh. My brother's name is Danny. They never get it right. Can't they tell the difference? He's been in high school for 2 years already, and they're still calling me by his name. I'm me! I'm totally different from Danny!"

As teachers, we have all referred to a younger sibling by the older child's name. Frustrating for the child, certainly, but not harmful if it is only a slip of the tongue. Much more detrimental to the young person is anticipating that Josh will learn in the same manner as Danny. If we anticipate that the younger brother or sister learns in the same manner as the older, we elevate the misidentification from a misdemeanor to "professional" misconduct. Believing that a child learns in one way when, in fact, the learner uses another set of approaches can prove truly frustrating and damaging to the child's sense of self as a learner.

Our greatest challenge as teachers is to acquaint ourselves with the mind of the learner by seeking to answer, "Who is this learner sitting in my classroom? What can I do to help his or her learning take place?"

The Learning Forces Within the Mind

If you really want to understand the learner, then you need to ask questions and listen intently to the answers. Listen for the voice. Isn't that the point of the previous chapter? But what are the right questions to ask? How can a teacher become familiar with the voice and the mind of the learner? Where can I begin to get the most direct answer to "Who is the me?" whom the learner brings to the classroom?

The Mind, the Message, the Voice of the Learner

To find the answer to who the learner is, you need to know what is going on in the learner's mind when learning is occurring. Now, that's a tall order. Actually, it's rather humbling to even ponder the answer. Yet this is the central question to all teaching-learning communication.

Cognitive Processes

Thinking, processing, communicating, firing neurons, releasing chemicals, associating, sorting, and sensing are all things that are going on in the learner's brain when learning is occurring. In fact, these activities are all a part of the cognitive "taking in" of the world around us.

As soon as students hear an assignment, they begin asking themselves, "Have I done an assignment like this before?" Their minds begin racing, sorting through their previous experiences and looking for a match. What we call transfer or association is that cognitive action that provides us with a recollection of previous learning that is very similar to the new learning being asked of us. When we are able to transfer previous experience into the current situation, we have a road map for digesting the assignment and thinking through how to respond to it.

We use our senses to take in and absorb the stimuli—the words, sounds, sights, smells, and touch of the learning task. We rely on our intelligences to transmit and translate for us what is happening in the external world and bring it into the internal world of our learning. We seek to use our myriad of intelligences—our thinking, analyzing, assessing mechanism to understand the words, numbers, pictures, music, motion, communication, and thoughts that are bouncing around inside our cognitive mechanism.

What is happening in our mind is a convergence of the past learning with the unknowns of the new learning. We are calling up previous experiences, exercising our memory, and at the same time building connectors and bridges through association to the new learning, that is, the unknown played against the backdrop of the known. The more experiences and the more associations, the stronger the linkage to previous learning. The greater the use of the senses and intelligences, the more likely the processing will develop a new understanding. The cognitive voice is the sifter of information and experience—the executive office of the brain that contains the rational and thought center of learning.

Conative Behaviors

At the same time that the cognitive processing is occurring, the brain is also determining what action to take to make learning work. This is the conative, or performance control center. Simultaneous to thinking, the brain is also preparing to act. Most frequently, the conative center determines the initial response to a learning assignment. It does so by determining "Should I flee from this task or take it on?" "Fight or flight" is what happens in the brain when the learner is first confronted with a task. This part of the learning experience can involve the release of chemicals in the brain that either energize or freeze a response to the learning challenge.

We ask, "So, what's so important about this? How can I use this now? What is its bottom-line benefit to me?" The litmus test is, "When will I ever use this outside of school?" And all the time, we are choosing how we want to proceed with the learning. Do we want to work alone? In groups? Away from others? In the midst of the action? That's our conative "autonomous factor" at work.

Our conative "pace factor" has us establishing the rate with which we are going to pursue the task. Do we want to move slowly and mull over what is happening? Do we want to charge in and get it done? Have we got the right tools with which to approach the task?

Is our toolkit equipped with a plan? Can we organize the activity before we proceed? Do we have the road map? The list of steps? Can we take our time and go step-by-step, checking off our list of "to do's" as we go?

Do we have the handbook? The text of information? Do we have the right terminology? Do we have our paper and pencil? Our record of the facts? Information? Data?

Do we have a means of figuring out what we are expected to do to complete the learning? Do we have the space to make the assignment make sense? Do we have a place to go and tinker with the problem?

Do we have the ideas that will make our action explode with "Wows"? Do we have our lifeboats and safety nets in place so that we can jump off from the known into the unknown and not crash and burn?

In other words, are we equipped to implement our thoughts and perform our learning operations in a successful manner? The conative performance activity of learning is the one aspect of each student's learning process that we can see within the classroom setting. Although we aren't privileged to be able to observe the cognitive memory search or the analysis and synthesis processes of a student's brain, we are able to observe the conative "doing" part of each learner's brain operations.

The problem is that we often miss the significance of the outward behavior of learning. We may even misinterpret it. For example, if a learner receives an assignment and appears to ignore it or not respond to it, we, as teachers, become concerned. Frustrated. Maybe even infuriated. Then, we become punitive. We don't hear the voice of the learner in the midst of our frustration with the student's response. What we interpret as a lack of response may actually be the wait time during which the student is choosing whether to flee or take on the assignment. Legitimate reasons for fleeing might be that the student (a) has done a similar assignment and didn't succeed, (b) doesn't believe the assignment has any relationship to the real world, or (c) doesn't believe he or she is equipped with the tools needed to begin or complete the assignment successfully. Reasons for staying and taking on the fight or challenge of learning something new are the countermands of the above.

If we misinterpret the pantomime of conative learning behaviors, we also miss the message, the voice of the learner. We think that the message being sent is one of defiance or stubbornness when, instead, the learner is relying on his or her need to get inside himself or herself and take the assignment into another place—away from the confinement of the classroom and classmates to a place where the learner can take the assignment apart and put it back together in a way that makes sense to him or her. We might misinterpret the learner's roaming the classroom, talking to classmates, checking on their progress, and talking about what to do and how to do it as being too sociable, unfocused, and distracting. If we were to label the behavior as such, we would miss the message that says "I need to work with others to make this assignment make sense."

The conative voice of learning is the most observable but not the most articulate. It is a drumbeat, a Morse code, a tapping of the pencil, a scraping of the desk, a staring out the window, an action-oriented means of communication—the choreography of learning rather than the lyrics. The message is there, loud and clear, and even though the voice is different, the communication is audible to the trained listener.

Affective Sense of Self

The brain also employs its affective, emotive sensors to the learning process. Here again, the teacher can identify the message by observing the expressiveness of the learner vis-à-vis the learning task. The cognitive brain function has just finished running a computer match to the assignment; the conative function has moved into action, figuring out the learning challenge and developing a plan by which to complete the assignment without taking too many risks. The affective, sensory portion of the brain, simultaneous to these brain functions, is responding to cognitive and conative brain activity.

The central issue to the affective response is, "How successful was I the last time I did this?" The operative word is *successful*. There is no doubt that the old adage is true: "Success does breed success." This is especially true in terms of the learner. When a learner successfully completes a learning task, the learner's brain actually experiences a high. Endorphins are released that give the learner a sense of achievement. It is this sense of accomplishment that the learner then carries into the next learning experience. Success pumps up the learner's energy level and prepares the learner to take on the next challenge.

This sense of success is not only intrinsic but also extrinsic. When learners receive positive feedback from peers and adults who are significant in their lives, they store in their cognitive processing the memory of this achievement, as well as the tools used to achieve this level of performance. The student's sense of self as a capable learner is increased, and the learner is ready to take on the next challenge.

Keeping the Mind Company

Hearing the affective voice of the learner is not difficult. Tolerating, interpreting, and responding to this part of the learner's means of communicating can be a real challenge. Often, teachers find themselves irritated and frustrated with the whining voice of the "I can't do this" learner, the "I don't understand this" declaration of the learner, or the "Why do we have to do this?" challenge from the learner. They turn off to the voice of the learner just at the point when the mind of the learner may well need the company of a teacher.

Within ourselves, we say that we don't have time to hear the anxiousness expressed by the student's quiet, nonresponsive presence. We don't want to contend with the defiant presence of the frustrated learner. We even limit the celebratory effusiveness of the successful learner. What we are doing, in effect, is telling the learner not to "feel," not to experience the emotions that are whirling inside. We are saying, "School is a place for taking in information and performing it; it is not a place to display emotions spontaneously. Leave those outside."

Don't be frustrated; just learn.

Don't be worried; just learn.

Don't be too happy; it distracts others from their learning.

If we truly believe that some minds need company, then the time to keep company is when the learner is struggling to overcome the pain of the previous failure, the defeat of the previous test, the fear of the new assignment, or the excitement of a recent revelation. It is also a time to respect the feelings of the learner and to respect the learner's need for space to work through the feelings he or she is experiencing.

Finding the Me of the Learner Within the Patterns of the Mind

We began this chapter by asking what is going on in the learner's mind when learning is occurring. The opening pages identified that brain activity manifests itself in the tri-partite functioning of the mind, that is, through the interaction of cognition, conation, and affectation. The basis of this three-part interaction is well established in both educational psychology and brain science. But simply understanding these interactions doesn't provide the voice of the learner with messages that can be understood by the teacher. What is needed is a means of explaining how these inter-actions of the mind converge to form identifiable learning behaviors.

Patterns of the Mind

The convergence of the three brain activities (cognition, conation, and affectation) form four stable patterns of learning, each with a distinct message. Taken together, they compose the learner's combination of learning voices. Each pattern exists in all of us to some degree and con-tributes to our unique learning combination (see Exhibit 2.1).

The Sequential Pattern

The sequential pattern expresses itself most clearly as, "I want clear direc-tions. Tell me what to do." This aspect of our learning seeks to follow step-by-step directions, organize and plan work carefully, and complete the assignment from beginning to end free from interruptions. The sequen-tial pattern is the "making connections" part of our learning.

Cognitively, it processes the world around us by looking for the match, the pattern, the previous experience, and comparing it to the new. The cognitive part of our sequential pattern has us running mental com-puter matches, flipping the file cards in milliseconds, identifying where we have seen or heard this before, and fitting the match into the great matrix of our mental storage capacity.

Conatively, it acts by organizing the stimulus into the correct catego-ries—drawing associations and creating new files, new directories. As a result, we list, organize, plan, and look for examples of what we did before; we follow the directions carefully in order to structure our learning; and we look for a way to work without interruptions that could break our line of concentration.

Affectively, it causes us to feel good about the learning task when we have proceeded in an organized manner to identify the linkage between this stimulus and prior encounters with similar stimuli (words, sights, sounds, tactile experiences, etc.). Our confidence to proceed comes from relying on what is known and how it relates to the new task. If we are able to see the match, we can organize our thoughts and plan how to deal with this learning experience. If we are not able to see the match or are rushed and not allowed to use this pattern to the degree we need to, we develop a fear of failure that inhibits successful performance of the learning task.

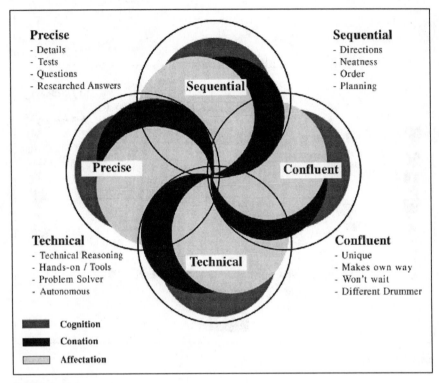

Precise
- Details
- Tests
- Questions
- Researched Answers

Sequential
- Directions
- Neatness
- Order
- Planning

Technical
- Technical Reasoning
- Hands-on / Tools
- Problem Solver
- Autonomous

Confluent
- Unique
- Makes own way
- Won't wait
- Different Drummer

Cognition
Conation
Affectation

Exhibit 2.1

If we recognize that this assignment is similar to another at which we did not succeed, then we require encouragement and assistance. It is in the latter two scenarios that the teacher's words of guidance, support, and thoughtful directions are needed.

The Precise Pattern

The precise pattern expresses itself as "I want information. Tell me the facts." It enables us to seek and process detailed information carefully and accurately. When using precision, the learner takes detailed notes, asks questions to find out more information, knows exact answers, and reads and writes in a highly specific manner. The precise pattern is our discovery pattern—it wants to know things with certainty.

Cognitively, it wants to have an explanation for how our world operates. It looks at the stimulus and asks, "How can you help explain the world to me?" It raises "If so, then what?" questions. It challenges what is heard and seen by comparing the new information to previous information—it seeks proof, asking, "Why should I replace my current understanding

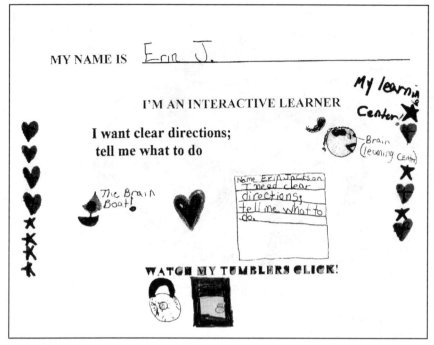

Exhibit 2.2

with this new explanation?" The precise pattern relies heavily on our memory or our notes.

Conatively, this pattern acts upon the new stimulus by questioning its validity. It is the confronter of our knowledge. It questions, challenges, analyzes, and corrects. It looks at all sides and leaves no stone unturned. It is constantly seeking more information, more facts, more data. It searches for accuracy in explanations, answers, and definitions. Conative actions manifest themselves in exact measurements and use of specific terms. They are heard in the careful and cautious qualification of statements by those who seek exacting communication. The precise pattern has us act upon the stimulus around us by capturing it. We record it—through writing, audiotapes, and videotapes. We document, we test, we prove we are right.

Affectively, this is our correct answer, perfection central. It is here that we feel affirmed in our "knowing." We take pride in the number of correct answers. We feel good when we have had the time to download our knowledge. It is our highly visible power base of learning because it is the most observable: we listen for the correct answer, we look for the correct answer. Unfortunately, teachers think that this is what learning is all about. We convince our students that communicating or repeating the facts we

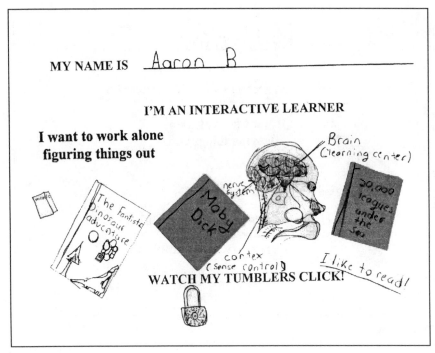

MY NAME IS _Aaron B_

I'M AN INTERACTIVE LEARNER

I want to work alone figuring things out

Brain
(learning center)

nerve system

Moby Dick

20,000 leagues under the sea

cortex
(sense control)

WATCH MY TUMBLERS CLICK!

The Fantastic Dinosaur adventure

I like to read!

Exhibit 2.3

have told them demonstrates their learning. So, learners seek to regurgitate information, falling victim to the trap that correct answers equal knowledge and understanding.

The Technical Pattern

The technical pattern's voice simply states, "I like to work alone figuring things out." This is the practical, relevance-seeking part of our learning. It is our nonverbal, "grab hold and do," move and shape, reconfigure, see-what-makes-it-work part of us. Through this learning pattern, we see the mechanics of operations, the function of pieces; we construct, we mull, we make it work, we get it done. This is where we learn autonomously, "hands-on," unencumbered by paper-and-pencil requirements. The technical pattern is our "actions speak louder than words" pattern.

Cognitively, this pattern engages our thinking around a series of questions all dealing with the issue of relevance. The questions we use to process this pattern are "What is the problem here?" and "What information do I need to correct this problem?" This pattern uses written information on an as-needed basis only. I don't need labels, words, or the correct form

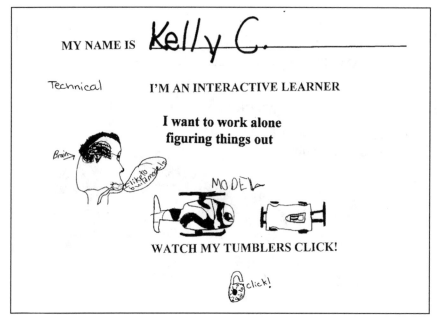

MY NAME IS **Kelly C.**

Technical   **I'M AN INTERACTIVE LEARNER**

**I want to work alone
figuring things out**

WATCH MY TUMBLERS CLICK!

Exhibit 2.4

of the written word. Instead, I need firsthand involvement. This is the most cognitively concrete of our learning patterns.

Conatively, this pattern has us seek elbow room and time to ourselves to solve the learning task, find solutions, and tinker with the mechanics of it. Through this pattern, we take charge of situations, wrestle with problems, tackle the tough jobs, and "get in and get it done!" This pattern, when used to a high degree, manifests itself physically in the building and repairing, inventing and constructing of items. Those who use this as their primary learning process revel in gadgets, gizmos, and machinery—all hands-on representations of how the world works.

Affectively, it is through this pattern that we develop our confidence in our ability to figure out the world around us and how it "ticks." This is the pattern that tests our sense of self-sufficiency. Interestingly, the only people to whom that seems to matter is ourselves, for it is in this pattern of our learning that we play things close to the vest. We are a "hard read" when using our technical processing. We are absorbed in solving what is in front of us and in overcoming that challenge. Affectively, this pattern is our most personal dimension, where the outcome is only important to us.

Within the technical pattern, we find the "marine factor," that is, "still waters run deep." Feelings of satisfaction in this pattern come when we've risen to the challenge and solved the situation; when we've tackled the problem and wrestled it to the ground. We've conquered it; we've defeated

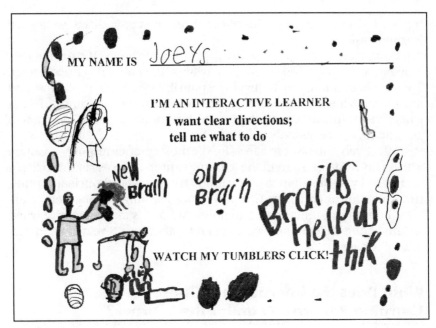

Exhibit 2.5

it; we've built and fashioned it, carved out a niche; and we've done it well. We feel especially confident when, as a result of our use of this pattern, there stands a physical representation of our technical prowess.

The Confluent Pattern

The confluent pattern of our learning combination shouts, "I want to make my ideas come to life!" This portion of our learning has us avoid conventional approaches and seek unique ways to complete any learning task. This is the part of our learning pattern that gives us permission to start before all directions are given; take a risk, fail, and start again; use imaginative ideas and unusual approaches; and improvise. The confluent pattern envisions beyond what is evident and carries the learner to the edge of his or her experiences and beyond.

Cognitively, this pattern allows the learner to hear what hasn't yet been spoken, see what has yet to be drawn, and read what has yet to be written. This pattern encourages the learner to read between the lines and intuit the big picture of what is being learned. The cognitive processing of confluence forms the glue of learning. It brings the disparate pieces of directions, minutiae, and problems together into a wholeness of insight. More than organizing, knowing, or figuring out, this pattern allows the learner to process the learning task through a unique set of lenses, enabling the learner to bring a new insight to a rather standardized, well-worn learning task.

Conatively, this pattern is always pushing the limits. It risks, it dares, it defies convention. This is our "I'm willing to try anything once" factor. This is where our ability to juggle responsibilities, tasks, problems, and assignments lies. Before we finish one task, we begin two others. This is where we venture into many things, finishing none of them. The goal is to get started, not necessarily to finish.

Affectively, this pattern allows for the most carefree responses. Failure is taken in stride as a part of the learning venture. Success in this pattern is marked by the freedom to risk, fail, and try again—without fear of punitive sanctions or criticism. This part of our learning development is the most celebratory, unfettered, and unbounded. It is most operative when we are young children and least operative after only 3 years in a formal school setting.

What Does the Interaction of These Learning Patterns Mean for the Learner?

The existence of the interactive patterns within the learner requires each to be able to start at a point that is "graspable." Each uses the voice of the dominant learning pattern(s) as the place to launch the learning task. Some may start by using their technical pattern. This means starting at a concrete, hands-on, "let's figure this out" level. It's OK if you tinker with it and get it to make some sense. It's OK to ask, "How am I going to use this? What good is this going to do me? When will I ever see this again?"

A learner might begin by using the confluent pattern, freely associating with the learning experience, dreaming, imagining, and playing with what's there; having fun with the possibilities; generating lots of approaches; and not being concerned with doing it in the way the teacher describes.

When the learner begins by using the sequential pattern, the learner usually begins by looking for a link to previous learning, asking to see examples, asking to go over the directions or for additional directions, or double-checking with someone "in the know" before proceeding with the task.

Learners who begin by using the precise pattern begin by asking, "What do I already know about this? Is what I am hearing and seeing accurate compared with what I already know? Do I remember this from before? What's the most up-to-date information? What are the new words? Terms? Can I wrap them around my tongue? Can I say them, spell them accurately? Will they give me more options for showing what I know?"

These are examples of a single pattern by which we begin our learning. Added to these are companion patterns, backup patterns, and pat-

Priority One

Sequential messages:

What are the directions? This looks a lot like what I did earlier this year, but it has some more steps to follow now. I can do this. I'm pretty sure. I don't need to give up and be worried.

Priority Two

Precise messages:

What do I already know about this? Is what I am hearing and seeing accurate compared with what I already know about this?

Nonprioritized

Technical and Confluent messages:

I need time to play with this new piece of learning and see where that leads. I need a concrete, hands-on, "let's figure this out" level. Wow! What an opportunity to do what I want to do! I have lots of ideas I'd like to try.

Exhibit 2.6

terns that we avoid altogether. It is the mixture of these interactive patterns—all acting simultaneously within the blink of an eye—that results in our learning. (And all this time, we teachers thought that all we had to do was tell students something new and demonstrate it for them, and they would be able to understand it.) Keep in mind that these activities are being used within us to differing degrees.

For example, if a learner uses the sequential pattern first, the precise pattern second, and avoids listening to the messages of his or her confluent and technical patterns, the actual mixture and priority of the messages occurring will be similar to those represented in Exhibits 2.6 and 2.7.

The questions or messages that arise midway through the assignment reflect the quieter voice of the precise pattern. The voice of the technical and confluent patterns remain silent because, in the case of this learner, these are patterns that this individual actually avoids.

The learner's mind is abuzz with these messages—awhirl with these patterns. What is encouraging about all of this insight is that when learners understand these patterns about themselves, they can begin to talk to their teacher about what is happening inside of them. When confronted with new learning, repetitious learning, project assignments, research assignments, writing assignments, or vocabulary assignments, these learners can identify what is preventing progress and why they are getting off track. A partnership develops, bringing the teacher and learner to a new

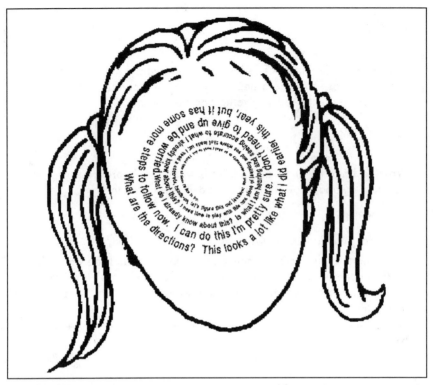

Exhibit 2.7

understanding of learning. The teacher will be able to hear the voice of the learner and understand what is being communicated. The learner will hear the voice of the teacher and recognize that they are in this learning experience together!

What's a Teacher to Do?

The question arises again: What does this mean for the teacher? It means that we need to be constantly asking ourselves, "What am I asking the learner to do when I am teaching math, science, reading, history, biology, social studies?" I need to be constantly on alert when introducing something new and totally unknown to the learner; I must think through what is being required of the learner.

This is when and where the teacher needs to be able to listen to the learner—to hear the words of concern or frustration, depersonalize the student's reaction to the learning task, and talk to the student about what is happening within him or her that is building barriers to success rather than pathways to learning. We need to listen to the sorting (sequential communication), sifting (precise communication), solving (technical action), and soaring (confluent communication) messages.

The importance of understanding these identifiable learning messages is made clear in the following anecdote:

> I planned carefully. I prepared diligently. Yet lesson after lesson I experienced the same response from students. Two minutes into the activity, Dale has his hand up asking the exact number of words I expect for each answer. Chris has started the assignment before I finished my explanation, and already I can see she's not following the directions. Gary, my quiet one, listened to the directions, but now is sitting with his notebook closed staring out the window totally disengaged. Five minutes into the lesson, Mardi is the only student on task. How is this possible? What happened to this well-planned lesson? (Johnston, 1997, p. 78)

Analyzing this anecdote, we quickly recognize two things: the lesson was well-planned, but well-planned lessons that, when implemented, are not in tune with the learner do not achieve the desired outcome. This is when the lesson becomes a wedge separating the learner from learning.

Before panic and frustration set in, it is important for the teacher to analyze what is occurring in this situation. It is far too early to abandon the plan or to declare the effort unsuccessful. The plan has just been announced. No teaching has occurred, no listening has occurred, and little learning has occurred. Telling doesn't equal knowing, doing, or succeeding. Learning is a process. It takes time. It takes opportunity for the learner to absorb, respond to, mull over, and consider what is being asked of him or her.

What the teacher in this anecdote is experiencing is healthy. The students are communicating to her. Now the task is for her to hear their message, read their signals, and keep working with them to keep their learning engaged. Remember, the learners in this classroom are still sorting, sifting, solving, and soaring. They are in the midst of asking themselves:

How will I begin this assignment?

Do I have enough information to begin?

How am I going to survive in this? When will I ever use this in the real world?

What's one way of completing this assignment that would be different from everyone else?

We need to remember that the introduction of the lesson is only the beginning of the learning interaction. Usually, the beginning of the lesson is composed of all "teacher talk." We ask the students a series of questions (our questions) that we believe should focus them on what we want them to learn. We disregard their questions. We want them to hear our information and follow our path of learning.

When We Listen Only to
Our Own Voice of Learning

Listening to our own voice of learning truly limits the manner in which we teach and the expectations that we set for others. After all, we know the information because we learned it when we prepared the lesson. We looked up the answers; we hold the information within us. We planned how to divide the lesson into pieces of activity and information based upon how it makes sense to us; next, we identified how we would check to see if the students are catching on—again based upon how we would like to be checked for our understanding—and finally, we planned the lesson based upon the pace with which we have absorbed the material and the manner in which we would best like to show or demonstrate what we have learned. Having spent hours in the preparation of the lesson, we deliver it to students in 20 to 40 minutes and expect them simply to accept our predigested learning.

Well, the fact is, real learners need the time, space, and opportunity to do their own person-specific learning. This means that they need at least the same amount of time to do the learning as we did to do the preparation of the lesson. They also need to make the learning their own. They need to be able to think about it, act upon it, and develop a sense of confidence in their ability to succeed in working with this new topic or project. When we plan lessons without this awareness, we ignore the interaction of the learner's cognition, conation, and affectation, imposing our own interactive learning. We also ignore the voice of the learner.

What Do We Hear When
We Listen to the Learner?

The first step in meeting the needs of learners is to understand how they learn—to recognize that organization, detailed information, problem solving, and risk taking are not natural learning behaviors for all students. The next step is to have students understand how they can make their unique learning patterns work for them!

As teachers, we can begin a dialogue of discovery with our students. Just a short time ago, a secondary school teacher and coach told me that his students were intrigued by the idea that their learning processes could be identified. "Once they saw how their results so accurately reflected what kind of learner they were, they were hooked. We are trying to make the connection of how this self-knowledge will benefit us all," he says. An unintended benefit resulted as well: "My students realize that I, as a teacher, actually do care about how they learn and who they are as individuals! I have gained their respect on another level, and it has nurtured our classroom relationships."

Who Is the "Me" in Let Me Learn?

The "me" in Let Me Learn is a unique set of learning patterns that makes each learner clever in his or her own way. Recognizing the voice of the learning patterns within each learner is vital. These skills and insights do not occur naturally or simply through experience. We need to be taught to be proficient in hearing the voice; translating its sorting, sifting, solving, and soaring messages; and applying the insights gained. Chapter 3 focuses on this next step, introducing the reader to the Learning Combination Inventory and its potential for identifying the "me" in Let Me Learn.

And This Is What They Said

The conative voice of learning is the most observable but not the most articulate. It is a drumbeat, a Morse code, a tapping of the pencil, a scraping of the desk, a staring out the window, an action-oriented means of communication—the choreography of learning rather than the lyrics. The message is there loud and clear, and even though the voice is different, the communication is audible to the trained listener.

C. JOHNSTON

References and Selected Bibliography

Bruer, J. (1997). Education and the brain: A bridge too far. *Educational Researcher, 26*(8), 4-16.

Churchland, P. (1995). *The engine of reason, the seat of the soul: A philosophical journey into the brain.* Cambridge: MIT Press.

Cohen, P. (1995). Understanding the brain. *Education Update, 37*(7).

Coleman, D. (1996). On emotional intelligence. *Educational Leadership, 54*(1), 6-11.

Corno, L. (1987). Teaching and self-regulated learning. In D. Berliner and B. Rosenshine, (Eds.), *Talks to teachers* (pp. 249-266). New York: Random House.

Eisner, E. (1997). Cognition and representation: A way to pursue the American dream? *Phi Delta Kappan, 78*(5), 349-360.

Gardner, H. (1995). A silence of a decade's length. *Phi Delta Kappan, 77,* 201-209.

Gibbs, N. (1995, October 2). The EO factor. *Time,* 60-68.

Hofstadter, D. (1995). *Fluid concepts and creative analogies.* New York: HarperCollins.

Johnston, C. (1996). *Unlocking the will to learn.* Thousand Oaks, CA: Corwin.

Johnston, C. (1997). Using the Learning Combination Inventory. *Educational Leadership, 55*(4), 78-82.

Kaikkonen, P. (1997). *Entwicklung der schulcultur: Perspektiven aus finnisher sicht.* Presented at the annual meeting of the European Conference on Educational Research, Frankfurt, Germany.

MacBeath, J. (1997). Learning to be intelligent. *Education Journal, 14,* 13.

Nesser, U., et al. (1996). Intelligence: Knowns and unknowns. *American Psychologist, 51*(2), 77-101.

Sternberg, R. (1996). Myths, countermyths, and truths about intelligence. *Educational Researcher, 25*(2), 11-16.

Sternberg, R., & Grigorenko, E. (1997). Are cognitive styles still in style? *American Psychologist, 52,* 700-712.

Further Reading

Caine, R., & Caine, G. (1991). *Making connections: Teaching and the human brain.* Arlington, VA: Association for Supervision and Curriculum Development.

Caine, R., & Caine, G. (1997). *Education on the edge of possibility.* Arlington, VA: Association for Supervision and Curriculum Development.

Educational Psychology Interactive: Systems Model of Human Behavior. [On-line]. Available: http://www.valdosta.edu/whuitt/psy702/sysmdlhb.html

Kucan, L., & Beck, I. (1997). Thinking aloud and reading comprehension research: Inquiry, instruction, and social interaction. *Review of Educational Research, 67,* 271-299.

Let Me Learn [On-line]. Available: http://www.letmelearn.org

Sylwester, R. (1995). *A celebration of neurons: An educator's guide to the human brain.* Arlington, VA: Association for Supervision and Curriculum Development.

Our schools should be . . . media for growing things, and what they should grow is our minds. They should try to achieve that noble ambition through . . . a way of life that recognizes both the differences and the commonalities among us.

Eisner, 1997, p. 349

3

What Is the Learning Combination Inventory?[1]

By human nature, we are a curious lot. We eagerly seek to learn about the world around us. Even more keen is our desire to know the future and what it holds for us. The Greeks sought the answer to this question by visiting the oracle at Delphi. Interestingly, the oracle was a woman, usually in her 50s, who chewed oregano leaves as a means of generating her skills of discernment. It is no wonder then, that, as a guidebook suggested, "Those who came to the oracle for help often left more bewildered than when they arrived."

The Maltese use the family ritual of *quccija* to see what the future holds for their children. This custom is carried out on a child's first birthday. The family places a number of objects on the floor across the room from the child. The items represent the parents' vocations or their hopes for the child. Whatever object the child grasps first is the one that predicts the child's future profession.

We may find these customs entertaining, but our rationale for dismissing their accuracy is simple: Neither of these approaches has validity or reliability. Interestingly, education's track record for using reliable and valid measures to determine who and what are the nature of learners is no more convincing than the international customs discussed above. The field of education is rife with learning instruments, ranging from self-report checklists of multiple intelligences to complex questionnaires yielding interpretive charts of geometric dimensions. Yet for years, educational and cognitive psychologists have voiced their concern over the lack of validation and reliability of these instruments.

As educators, we know that information is only as valid as the means used to collect and interpret it. No oracles, no games—just consistently accurate measures that provide a valid basis for understanding how a child learns.

Now if we take this a step further and apply it to listening to the voice of the learner, we are confronted with the questions: What is a valid and consistent means of hearing the voice of the learner? Can I visit with the learner and, by listening, understand all I need to know? Can I observe the learner and draw conclusions from my observations? Will this prove a valid means of hearing the voice? The answer to these questions is, simply, "No."

To have a valid understanding of who the learner is and what the message is, a teacher needs an objective means of collecting the information and interpreting it that is free from personal biases and distractions. The Learning Combination Inventory (LCI), developed using 6 years of pilot studies with U.S. and international students, is an instrument that has achieved this goal.

The LCI's strength lies in its ability to identify, accurately and consistently, an individual's hard-wired learning patterns. These patterns, as described in Chapter 2, are the result of cognitive, conative, and affective brain functions that are present from birth and developed over time. To understand what this means, the reader needs to "experience" the LCI. Thus, the remainder of this chapter explains the LCI and how to interpret its outcomes. This chapter is intended to be informative about the instrument—how it works and what insights it can provide. The reader will find many examples of professionals from all walks of life who have completed the LCI as well as dozens of examples of school-age children's responses.

The examples of school-age learners' responses confirm the universality of the learning patterns. This is verified in the "Echo Voice" section of this chapter, where learners from different cultures and of different ages describe their learning frustrations in virtually the same words. The point is clear: The voice of the learner is a distinct voice with a clear message—a message that is powerful and forthright. It needs only to be captured, amplified, and listened to.

The Learning Combination Inventory (Professional Form)

Exhibit 3.1 is a facsimile of the Professional Form of the LCI developed for use with adults. Take a few minutes to complete the inventory, and be certain to respond to the open-ended questions found at the end of the 28 statements. After responding to the statements and writing the answers to the questions, transfer the responses to the score sheet provided in Exhibit 3.2. Remember, the results are only as accurate as the forthrightness with which you respond to the statements and questions. You are encour-
~d to use the full breadth of the scale to achieve the clearest result. For
~ost accurate results, complete the LCI before reading further.

What's My Learning Combination?

The results of the LCI are first reported in a sequence of scores labeled Sequence, Precision, Technical, and Confluent Processing. The scores within each scale are divided into ranges (i.e., 7-16 = I avoid this pattern, 17-25 = I use this pattern as needed, and 26-35 = I use this pattern first). The degree of variation among the scores, the placement of the scores within a given range, and the combination of the scores all provide insights into the "volume" of the voice of each learning pattern.

A unique feature of the LCI is the internal validity check provided by the written responses. Not only is the content of what is written important, but so is the amount. Both provide valuable insights into the learner's use of learning tools and sense of self. Using a standard set of written protocols, established during the first 3 years of plotting the instrument, the user can determine whether the written responses support the scale scores.

For example, if the scale score of Sequence Processing falls in the "I Use This First" 26-35 range and the written response to Question 1 (What frustrates you about an assignment?) reads, "The thing that frustrates me is when I don't have clear directions," "I need to see a sample of the work before I begin," "Learning should be done in a format like outlines. It should be neat and organized," or "I like step-by-step directions," then what is written validates the scale score for sequence.

If the scale score for Precise Processing falls between 26-35, the answer to "How would you show what you know?" will usually include a reference to taking a test, taking a quiz, or writing an essay or research paper. The written answers of those who use the Precise Pattern to a high degree are usually longer and more detailed than the answers written by others.

If the scale score for Technical Processing falls between 26-35, the written answers may be very brief, and what is written is straight to the point. "I want to work hands-on." "Let me demonstrate what I know." "I don't like to do a lot of writing." "Let me tell you one-on-one." "Let me show you out in the real world."

If the scale score for Confluent Processing is in the 26-35 range, the written response will typically contain references to taking risks, using unique ideas, trying something new, doing it your own way, or seeing something from an entirely new perspective—the big picture!

Of course, just looking at the "I Use This First" scores tells only part of the learning combination. The voice of the learner becomes even more articulate as the "I Use as Needed" and "I Avoid" messages are analyzed. In combining the 28 items with the three open-ended questions, the LCI

1. I would rather build a project than read or write about a subject.
   Never   Almost Never   Sometimes   Almost Always   Always

2. I need clear directions that tell me what is expected of me before I begin a task.
   Never   Almost Never   Sometimes   Almost Always   Always

3. I just enjoy generating lots of unique and creative ideas.
   Never   Almost Never   Sometimes   Almost Always   Always

4. I instinctively correct others whose information or answers are not totally accurate.
   Never   Almost Never   Sometimes   Almost Always   Always

5. I feel better when I have time to double check my work.
   Never   Almost Never   Sometimes   Almost Always   Always

6. I like to take things apart to see how they work.
   Never   Almost Never   Sometimes   Almost Always   Always

7. I am interested in knowing detailed information about whatever I am studying.
   Never   Almost Never   Sometimes   Almost Always   Always

8. I like coming up with a totally new and different way of doing an assignment instead of doing it the same way as everybody else.
   Never   Almost Never   Sometimes   Almost Always   Always

9. I look for well-documented, factual articles to read.
   Never   Almost Never   Sometimes   Almost Always   Always

10. I keep a neat desk or work area.
    Never   Almost Never   Sometimes   Almost Always   Always

11. I like to work with hand tools, power tools, and gadgets.
    Never   Almost Never   Sometimes   Almost Always   Always

12. I am willing to risk offering new ideas even in the face of discouragement.
    Never   Almost Never   Sometimes   Almost Always   Always

13. I need to have a complete understanding of the directions before I feel comfortable doing an assignment.
    Never   Almost Never   Sometimes   Almost Always   Always

14. I correct typos and inaccurate information in the printed materials I read.
    Never   Almost Never   Sometimes   Almost Always   Always

t 3.1 Learning Combination Inventory

15. I like hands-on assignments where I get to use mechanical/ technical instruments.
    Never   Almost Never   Sometimes   Almost Always   Always

16. I become frustrated when I have to wait patiently for someone to finish giving instructions.
    Never   Almost Never   Sometimes   Almost Always   Always

17. I prefer to build things by myself without anyone's guidance.
    Never   Almost Never   Sometimes   Almost Always   Always

18. I become frustrated if directions are changed while I'm working on a task.
    Never   Almost Never   Sometimes   Almost Always   Always

19. I pride myself in giving factually correct answers to the questions I am asked.
    Never   Almost Never   Sometimes   Almost Always   Always

20. I don't like having to do my work in one way, especially when I have a better idea I would like to try.
    Never   Almost Never   Sometimes   Almost Always   Always

21. I clean up my work area and put things back where they belong as soon as I finish a job.
    Never   Almost Never   Sometimes   Almost Always   Always

22. I enjoy the challenge of fixing or building something.
    Never   Almost Never   Sometimes   Almost Always   Always

23. I react quickly to assignments and questions without thinking through my answers.
    Never   Almost Never   Sometimes   Almost Always   Always

24. I automatically take notes whenever I listen to a presentation.
    Never   Almost Never   Sometimes   Almost Always   Always

25. I ask more questions than most people because I just enjoy knowing things.
    Never   Almost Never   Sometimes   Almost Always   Always

26. I like to figure out how things work.
    Never   Almost Never   Sometimes   Almost Always   Always

27. I am told by others that I am very organized.
    Never   Almost Never   Sometimes   Almost Always   Always

28. I like to make up my own way of doing things.
    Never   Almost Never   Sometimes   Almost Always   Always

Exhibit 3.1 Continued

Short-answer responses:

1. What made assignments frustrating for me in school was:

_____

_____

_____

_____

2. If I could choose, I would show what I have learned by . . .

_____

_____

_____

_____

3. My most memorable and enjoyable learning experience involved . . .

_____

_____

_____

_____

Exhibit 3.1 Continued

is able to facilitate the expression of the learner's internalized learning pattern. After completing tests of construct, content, and internal validity, as well as reliability (test/retest) with more than 15,000 public, private, and college-age students, teachers, parents, and administrators across the United States and throughout Europe (Northern Ireland, England, 'taly, and the Republic of Malta), we know that these responses hold true
   ·ardless of age, gender, or classification as a learner!

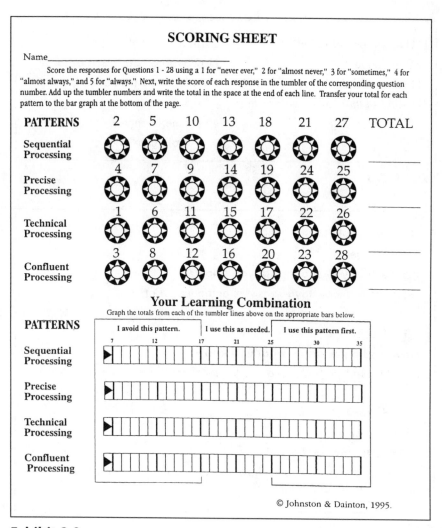

SCORING SHEET

Name_____

Score the responses for Questions 1 - 28 using a 1 for "never ever," 2 for "almost never," 3 for "sometimes," 4 for "almost always," and 5 for "always." Next, write the score of each response in the tumbler of the corresponding question number. Add up the tumbler numbers and write the total in the space at the end of each line. Transfer your total for each pattern to the bar graph at the bottom of the page.

PATTERNS	2	5	10	13	18	21	27	TOTAL
Sequential Processing								_____
	4	7	9	14	19	24	25	
Precise Processing								_____
	1	6	11	15	17	22	26	
Technical Processing								_____
	3	8	12	16	20	23	28	
Confluent Processing								_____

Your Learning Combination

Graph the totals from each of the tumbler lines above on the appropriate bars below.

PATTERNS — I avoid this pattern. | I use this as needed. | I use this pattern first.

- Sequential Processing
- Precise Processing
- Technical Processing
- Confluent Processing

© Johnston & Dainton, 1995.

Exhibit 3.2

What's Their Learning Combination?

Professional/Work World

One of the most interesting things we have learned as we have continued to gather examples of learning combinations is that adult learners' patterns are not any different from school-age learners'. They are as variable

"Use Sequential First"   27 in Sequential

30 in Sequential   **How would you teach others?**

How would you teach others?   *I would do my plan of action.*

I would sit them all down and tell   • Summarizing
them step by step.   • Experimenting
                                        • Evaluation after each lesson

Exhibit 3.3

"Use Precise First"

30 in Precise

How would you show what you know?

Do a test and look up the answers and get an A on it.

30 in Precise

How would you show what you know?

I would take time and prove it to the teacher.

"Avoid Precise"

15 in Precise

What is frustrating?

I get frustrated like when we have research and I don't find any information. I find it boring.

Exhibit 3.4

and distinct as each child's. There is no one single professional profile that predicts success! What does become obvious, however, is that the patterns of professionals closely match the demands of their professional vocation. Look through the following gallery of sample score sheets and note the match between patterns and profession.

"Use Confluent First"

32 in Confluent

How would you teach others?

I would encourage unique ways of doing things.

35 in Confluent and 27 in Sequential

How would you show what you know?

I would join unique ideas together in groups.

Exhibit 3.5

"Use Technical First"

29 in Technical

How would you show what you know?

I would just tell the teacher what I know without writing or tests.

35 in Technical

How would you show what you know?

I would build or demonstrate something.

Exhibit 3.6

text continues on page 67

PATTERNS	2	5	10	13	18	21	27	TOTAL
Sequential Processing	(5)	(5)	(4)	(5)	(5)	(5)	(5)	34
	4	7	9	14	19	24	25	
Precise Processing	(4)	(4)	(5)	(5)	(5)	(4)	(3)	30
	1	6	11	15	17	22	26	
Technical Processing	(3)	(3)	(3)	(3)	(2)	(3)	(3)	20
	3	8	12	16	20	23	28	
Confluent Processing	(3)	(2)	(3)	(3)	(4)	(2)	(4)	21

Part II: Please answer each of the following questions in your own words.

What makes assignments frustrating for you?

It becomes frustrating for me when the directions are unclear and not specific—there is a hidden assignment or agenda and when I am trying to figure out what the instructor really wants.

If you could choose, what would you do to show what you have learned?

I'd like to give a demonstration to show what I have learned.

My most memorable and enjoyable learning experience involved . . .

My most memorable learning experience involved play-acting. It occurred in a psychology class. I could see how a person reacted. It was fun. In one situation we play-acted different students coming into the school nurse's office.

Exhibit 3.7 School Nurse

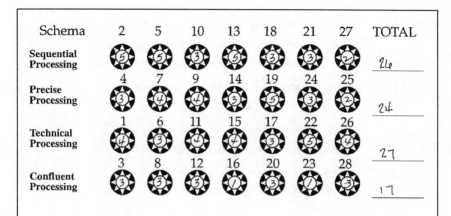

Schema	2	5	10	13	18	21	27	TOTAL
Sequential Processing	⑤	⑤	③	⑤	③	③	②	26
	4	7	9	14	19	24	25	
Precise Processing	③	④	④	③	⑤	③	②	24
	1	6	11	15	17	22	26	
Technical Processing	④	③	④	④	③	⑤	④	27
	3	8	12	16	20	23	28	
Confluent Processing	③	③	③	①	③	①	③	17

Part II: Please answer each of the following questions in your own words.

What makes assignments frustrating for you?

Unclear/ambiguous instruction and directions. Interrupting.

If you could choose, what would you do to show what you have learned?

Nothing really. It's not important to me to outwardly demonstrate to others. Inward satisfaction is sufficient.

My most memorable and enjoyable learning experience involved . . .

Exhibit 3.8 Banker

Schema	2	5	10	13	18	21	27	TOTAL
Sequential Processing	②	②	②	②	③	③	③	17
	4	7	9	14	19	24	25	
Precise Processing	④	⑤	⑤	①	⑤	④	④	28
	1	6	11	15	17	22	26	
Technical Processing	④	④	⑤	⑤	⑤	⑤	⑤	33
	3	8	12	16	20	23	28	
Confluent Processing	⑤	⑤	⑤	④	⑤	④	④	32

Part II: Please answer each of the following questions in your own words.

What makes assignments frustrating for you?

It is frustrating when there is only "one way" to do something. It is frustrating to do something according to another's methods when I see a better way.

If you could choose, what would you do to show what you have learned?

Simply "do it," but do it in an appropriate and efficient manner—whatever "it" may be. I don't need to show anyone.

My most memorable and enjoyable learning experience involved . . .

My professional education as a whole from "Tell-show-do" to "watch one-do one-teach one." Teaching is a valuable learning experience, because it keeps you on your toes.

Exhibit 3.9 Dentist

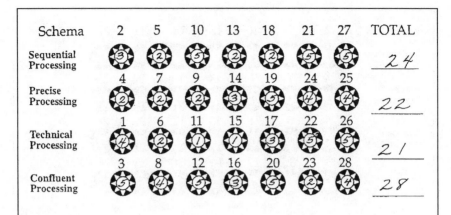

Part II: Please answer each of the following questions in your own words.

What makes assignments frustrating for you?

Too narrow of an area for action and very limited time periods to respond.

If you could choose, what would you do to show what you have learned?

Through results and demonstrated outcomes.

My most memorable and enjoyable learning experience involved . . .

Understanding several areas of symbolic logic, mathematical sociology, and multi-variate statistical analysis.

Exhibit 3.10 University President

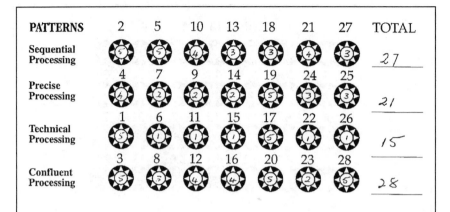

Part II: Please answer each of the following questions in your own words.

What makes assignments frustrating for you?

If there's an element in the assignment which I don't understand.

If you could choose, what would you do to show what you have learned?

I love to show what I know in an oral presentation. I rely on my vivid imagination for the employment of words.

My most memorable and enjoyable learning experience involved . . .

Working as the Ambassador has been the greatest, most wonderful learning experience.

Exhibit 3.11 Foreign Diplomat

Schema	2	5	10	13	18	21	27	TOTAL
Sequential Processing	④	③	③	⑤	③	④	③	25
	4	7	9	14	19	24	25	
Precise Processing	④	⑤	③	③	④	③	④	26
	1	6	11	15	17	22	26	
Technical Processing	③	④	④	④	③	④	④	25
	3	8	12	16	20	23	28	
Confluent Processing	④	③	④	③	③	②	④	23

Part II: Please answer each of the following questions in your own words.

What makes assignments frustrating for you?

It it is a subject that does not interest one and requires considerable reading research.

If you could choose, what would you do to show what you have learned?

Pass the knowledge on to others that may be interested in the subject. Use the knowledge to earn money.

My most memorable and enjoyable learning experience involved . . .

The responsibility of running a large textile mill 3 shifts 7 days per week. Involving—Production—Quality—Purchasing—Inventing—Union negotiations—Hiring personnel—Teaching the craft—Solving problems & seeing results. I learned a lot from this experience & enjoyed it.

Exhibit 3.12 Industrialist/Entreperneur

Schema	2	5	10	13	18	21	27	TOTAL
Sequential Processing	3	4	1	3	2	2	1	16
	4	7	9	14	19	24	25	
Precise Processing	4	5	5	4	5	3	2	28
	1	6	11	15	17	22	26	
Technical Processing	2	3	3	3	2	4	3	21
	3	8	12	16	20	23	28	
Confluent Processing	4	4	4	5	4	2	4	2>

Part II: Please answer each of the following questions in your own words.

What makes assignments frustrating for you?

If I am unable to locate the necessary background information or where to find that information to answer a question.

If you could choose, what would you do to show what you have learned?

Tell someone about it. I am especially fascinated by serendipitous things.

My most memorable and enjoyable learning experience involved . . .

Doing research on my family history/genealogy and realizing how little I really knew about history, both local and global.

Exhibit 3.13 Family-Practice Physician

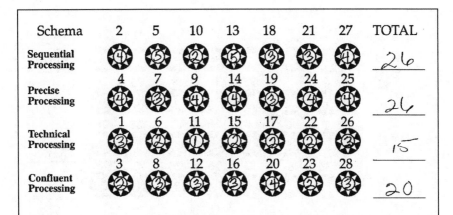

Schema	2	5	10	13	18	21	27	TOTAL
Sequential Processing	4	5	2	5	3	3	4	26
Precise Processing	4	3	4	4	3	4	4	24
Technical Processing	3	2	1	2	2	2	2	15
Confluent Processing	2	3	3	2	4	2	3	20

Part II: Please answer each of the following questions in your own words.

What makes assignments frustrating for you?

Assignments that do not have clear directions frustrate me. I also like to have clear definition of all that must be included in the assignments. Pressure to complete assignments in unrealistic amount of time also frustrates me.

If you could choose, what would you do to show what you have learned?

I would like to present a model or demonstration of what I have learned. I would like to do this with real children. I do *not* like writing long research papers.

My most memorable and enjoyable learning experience involved . . .

A studio art course in which we were free to create and use many different media.

Exhibit 3.14 Elementary School Teacher

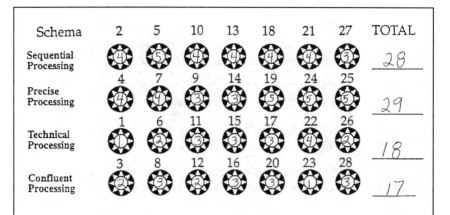

Schema	2	5	10	13	18	21	27	TOTAL
Sequential Processing	4	5	4	4	4	4	3	28
	4	7	9	14	19	24	25	
Precise Processing	4	4	3	3	5	5	5	29
	1	6	11	15	17	22	26	
Technical Processing	1	2	3	3	3	4	2	18
	3	8	12	16	20	23	28	
Confluent Processing	2	3	2	3	3	1	3	17

Part II: Please answer each of the following questions in your own words.

What makes assignments frustrating for you?

Time constraints and lack of direction frustrate me.

If you could choose, what would you do to show what you have learned?

I would make a presentation with supporting written materials, but an opportunity to orally explain.

My most memorable and enjoyable learning experience involved . . .

Working with others and sharing in a professional manner.

Exhibit 3.15 Secondary School Teacher

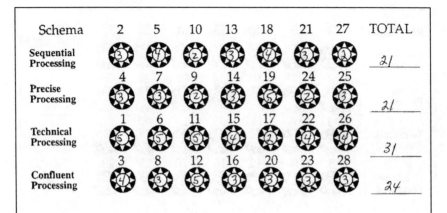

Schema	2	5	10	13	18	21	27	TOTAL
Sequential Processing	③	④	②	③	④	③	①	21
	4	7	9	14	19	24	25	
Precise Processing	③	③	②	③	⑤	②	③	21
	1	6	11	15	17	22	26	
Technical Processing	⑤	⑤	⑤	④	②	④	④	31
	3	8	12	16	20	23	28	
Confluent Processing	④	③	⑤	③	③	③	③	24

Part II: Please answer each of the following questions in your own words.

What makes assignments frustrating for you?

Not being able to get on with an assignment quick enough. And also being told what to do rather than being able to work things out myself.

If you could choose, what would you do to show what you have learned?

Talk about what I know, maybe with some practical examples, I'd be more confident speaking on one to one. But a group situation I could cope with.

My most memorable and enjoyable learning experience involved . . .

Traveling over seas. Seeing how other people do things and live.

Exhibit 3.16 Sheep-Shearing Champion of Wales

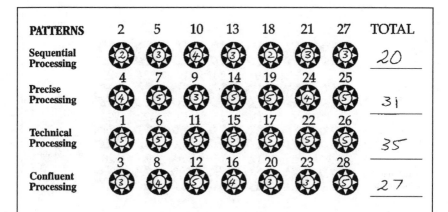

PATTERNS	2	5	10	13	18	21	27	TOTAL
Sequential Processing	2	3	4	3	2	3	3	20
Precise Processing	4	7	9	14	19	24	25	
	4	5	3	5	5	4	5	31
Technical Processing	1	6	11	15	17	22	26	
	5	5	5	5	5	5	5	35
Confluent Processing	3	8	12	16	20	23	28	
	3	4	5	4	3	3	5	27

Part II: Please answer each of the following questions in your own words.

What makes assignments frustrating for you?

No chance to do what I like.

If you could choose, what would you do to show what you have learned?

Have more hours of experience.

My most memorable and enjoyable learning experience involved . . .

Learning to play the tuba.

Exhibit 3.17 American Farmer

PATTERNS	2	5	10	13	18	21	27	TOTAL
Sequential Processing	⑤	⑤	⑤	⑤	③	⑤	②	30
	4	7	9	14	19	24	25	
Precise Processing	③	④	④	④	⑤	④	⑤	29
	1	6	11	15	17	22	26	
Technical Processing	③	③	③	⑤	③	④	④	25
	3	8	12	16	20	23	28	
Confluent Processing	③	③	⑤	②	③	③	③	22

Part II: Please answer each of the following questions in your own words.

What makes assignments frustrating for you?

Not having enough knowledge about the assignment and/or not having the materials to to the assignment.

If you could choose, what would you do to show what you have learned?

An answer and question class using examples and showing the "how too's."

My most memorable and enjoyable learning experience involved . . .

Another cashier when I was just starting out in the casino. She was training me in the Redemption area and she was very kind, pleasant and easy going. She made the new experience a fun and enjoyable event.

Exhibit 3.18 Former Sewing Machine Operator, Legal Secretary, and Casino Department Manager

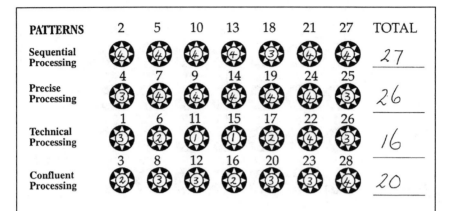

PATTERNS	2	5	10	13	18	21	27	TOTAL
Sequential Processing	④	④	④	④	③	④	④	27
	4	7	9	14	19	24	25	
Precise Processing	③	④	④	④	④	④	③	26
	1	6	11	15	17	22	26	
Technical Processing	③	②	①	①	②	④	③	16
	3	8	12	16	20	23	28	
Confluent Processing	②	③	③	②	③	③	④	20

Part II: Please answer each of the following questions in your own words.

What makes assignments frustrating for you?

> In driving—if I don't have a clear route. It is frustrating if children aren't sitting down and being quiet—so you can do your job.

If you could choose, what would you do to show what you have learned?

> I would demonstrate the proper way of driving. Do a course in Defensive Driving, and take a test after watching a video.

My most memorable and enjoyable learning experience involved . . .

> Learning to drive all the different buses, then learning all the lines and qualifying on these lines.

Exhibit 3.19 Transit Bus and School Bus Driver

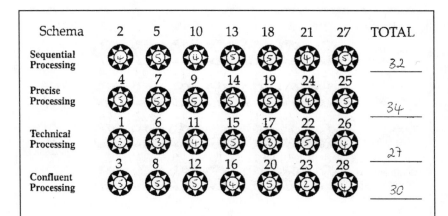

Schema	2	5	10	13	18	21	27	TOTAL
Sequential Processing	④	⑤	④	⑤	⑤	④	⑤	32
Precise Processing	4 ⑤	7 ⑤	9 ⑤	14 ⑤	19 ⑤	24 ④	25 ⑤	34
Technical Processing	1 ③	6 ③	11 ④	15 ⑤	17 ③	22 ⑤	26 ④	27
Confluent Processing	3 ⑤	8 ⑤	12 ⑤	16 ④	20 ⑤	23 ②	28 ④	30

Part II: Please answer each of the following questions in your own words.

What makes assignments frustrating for you?

The thing that frustrates me about assignments is that I arrive home at 3:45, I eat and I start my homework at 4:15. Before 7:30–8:00 I never finish. I never have time to watch tv or to go out, then we have to study for the exams. We shouldn't spend all that time on h.w. We should do more s.w. They never give us enough time to do the project, and we have to do everything at home.

If you could choose, what would you do to show your teacher what you have learned?

I would suggest that we should do examples after the new lessons of geography (example) the teacher does one or two lessons on revision and asks us some questions like a quiz. We shouldn't stay revising for tests, it's too frustrating. I think what I said above (about quizzes) because it is more fun and less tiring.

If you were the teacher, how would you have students learn?

If I was the teacher I wouldn't have people reading in class without sense because you never understand anything or you forget everything. I would do more outings and more plays and games. More discussions, less h.w., quizzes and stuff that the children have fun doing because like that they will look forward to the lesson and have fun and remember what we did in the lesson!

Exhibit 3.20 Malta Student, 13-Year-Old Female

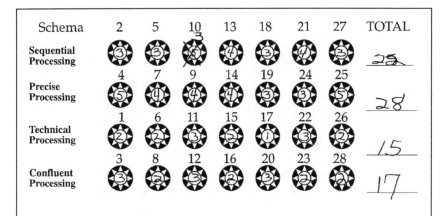

Schema	2	5	10	13	18	21	27	TOTAL
Sequential Processing	3	3	3	4	3	4	3	23
	4	7	9	14	19	24	25	
Precise Processing	5	4	4	4	3	3	5	28
	1	6	11	15	17	22	26	
Technical Processing	2	2	3	2	1	3	2	15
	3	8	12	16	20	23	28	
Confluent Processing	3	2	3	2	3	2	2	17

Part II: Please answer each of the following questions in your own words.

What makes assignments frustrating for you?

I don't like it when the teacher gives us lots of work and some are bad and we have to stay in from recess and then we get lots of homework and when I get home I have to do math and social studies and spelling and then I can't watch my favorite tv show.

If you could choose, what would you do to show your teacher what you have learned?

I would read a book and write about it and show her what I know about it.

If you were the teacher, how would you have students learn?

I would teach just like Mrs. H.

Exhibit 3.21 U.S. Student, 8-Year-Old Female

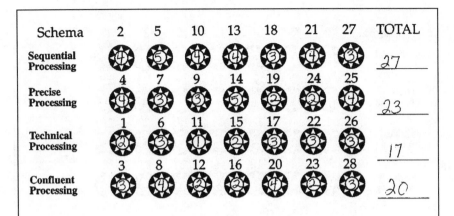

Schema	2	5	10	13	18	21	27	TOTAL
Sequential Processing	④	⑤	④	④	⑤	④	③	27
Precise Processing	④	③	③	⑤	②	②	④	23
Technical Processing	②	③	①	②	③	③	③	17
Confluent Processing	③	④	②	②	④	②	③	20

Part II: Please answer each of the following questions in your own words.

What makes assignments frustrating for you?

I do not like to do speaking or presentations. I want to know clear instructions and to have plenty of time to complete the assignment. If I do not know what is expected then I become frustrated.

If you could choose, what would you do to show what you have learned?

I would write about it. I would much rather describe in my own words what I know, and I do not like multiple choice.

My most memorable and enjoyable learning experience involved . . .

My sixth grade teacher read Charlie & the Chocolate Factory and told us you are never too old to read great literature.

Exhibit 3.22 U.S. Teacher, First Grade, Female

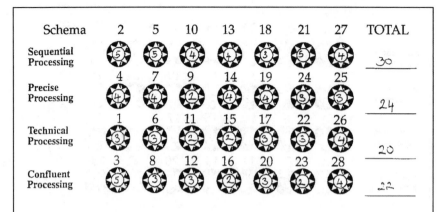

Schema	2	5	10	13	18	21	27	TOTAL
Sequential Processing	5	5	4	4	3	5	4	30
	4	7	9	14	19	24	25	
Precise Processing	4	4	2	4	4	3	3	24
	1	6	11	15	17	22	26	
Technical Processing	3	3	2	2	3	3	4	20
	3	8	12	16	20	23	28	
Confluent Processing	5	3	3	2	3	2	4	22

Part II: Please answer each of the following questions in your own words.

What makes assignments frustrating for you?

The time limit or lack of time. I need time to first organize well my ideas, and then starting the actual work.

If you could choose, what would you do to show what you have learned?

I will put down in my assignment things that the teacher might have said during the lesson and then reinforce the answer in my assignment by adding my own ideas.

My most memorable and enjoyable learning experience involved . . .

I would: create the best teaching env., develop the lesson as creative as possible, give my own examples and encourage them to give me theirs, reinforce them to ask questions whenever they have a difficulty, praise their work when its good and expecting better work when its poor, giving them material or tests which can develop on their own with little guidance. I believe that when a pupil succeeds in learning something with *little* guidance he will keep on remembering that thing.

Exhibit 3.23 Maltese Teacher, Eighth Grade, Female

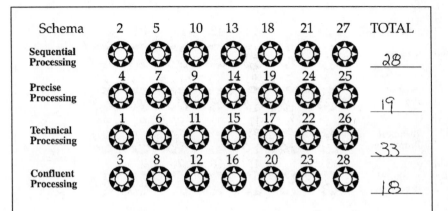

Schema	2	5	10	13	18	21	27	TOTAL
Sequential Processing								28
	4	7	9	14	19	24	25	
Precise Processing								19
	1	6	11	15	17	22	26	
Technical Processing								33
	3	8	12	16	20	23	28	
Confluent Processing								18

Part II: Please answer each of the following questions in your own words.

What makes assignments frustrating for you?

I don't like it when there are too many confusing directions and when the class is noise.

If you could choose, what would you do to show what you have learned?

If you want to know what I know come home with me and I'll show you what I can do.

My most memorable and enjoyable learning experience involved . . .

I would teach things really good and really teach them how to do it. I'd explain things until they really got it.

Exhibit 3.24 U.S. Special Needs Student, 11-Year-Old Male

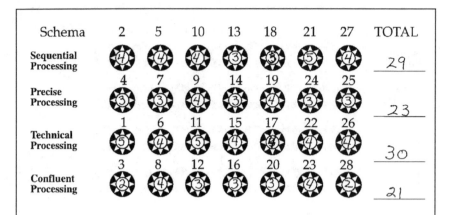

Schema	2	5	10	13	18	21	27	TOTAL
Sequential Processing	④	④	④	③	⑤	⑤	④	29
	4	7	9	14	19	24	25	
Precise Processing	③	③	④	③	④	③	③	23
	1	6	11	15	17	22	26	
Technical Processing	⑤	④	⑤	④	④	④	④	30
	3	8	12	16	20	23	28	
Confluent Processing	②	④	③	③	③	④	②	21

Part II: Please answer each of the following questions in your own words.

What makes assignments frustrating for you?

The teacher makes classroom learning hard for me by telling different groups of children to do different things. It becomes confusing. I really don't like distractions when I am trying to work.

If you could choose, what would you do to show what you have learned?

I hate doing any types of sums especially worksheets. I prefer to learn by watching demonstrations. I like to invent things. I could then show the teacher these things and she would realize what I know.

My most memorable and enjoyable learning experience involved . . .

I need to have someone who understands me to sit next to me and explain again exactly what I'm meant to do. So that is how I would teach.

Exhibit 3.25 UK Special Needs Student, 11-Year-Old Male

The Interaction of Precision and Technical Reasoning

18   26   32   18

R. A. (a teacher)

What is frustrating?

When you have to write a report with no references available.

How would you show what you know?

Projects would be the ideal for this and eliminate stress produced by tests.

How would you teach others?

Presentations, project works, without, however, eliminating tests and paperwork such as note taking.

Exhibit 3.26

Looking at the Scores and Missing the Voice

As educators, we have been trained to look at scores and interpret them on the basis of their numerical value, believing that the higher the score, the better the outcome. In the case of the LCI, that notion needs to be set aside. Setting it aside does not come easily. Beginning an interpretation of the LCI by looking for strengths and weaknesses is definitely a "schooling" approach, but not a "learner-centered" approach.

In the case of the LCI, to fixate on high scores is to ignore the mixture of all the scores *and* the uniqueness of the entire learning combination. It is the mixture of the range of the processes that a learner "Uses First" along with those the learner "Avoids," and followed by those "Used as Needed," that makes up the learner's unique learning combination.

There are strong differences and subtle differences among these mixtures. They are not difficult to see or understand once they have been explained to the person doing the score interpretation. However, they are vital to having an accurate interpretation of the learning combination and vital to the learner's and teacher's awareness and use of this information.

Listen to this interactive message of the individual depicted in Exhibit 3.26. This teacher-learner begins her learning by using her Technical Reasoning and Precision. She uses sequential and confluent processing only

The Interaction of Sequence, Precision, and Confluence

30   24   20   22

D. M. (a teacher)

What is frustrating?

I need time to first organize well my ideas before starting the actual work.

How would you show what you know?

I put down things that the teacher said and then reinforce the answer by adding my own ideas.

How would you teach others?

Develop the lesson creatively.

Give my own examples.

Encourage them to ask questions.

Exhibit 3.27

when needed. Consequently, she is frustrated when she doesn't have the factual resources (references) or the "tools" she needs to complete the assignment. Her responses to how she would show what she knows and how she would teach include obvious and balanced references to both issues of technical reasoning (projects and project works) and precision (not eliminating tests, paperwork, or notes). What we "hear" as we read this is the need to have sources of information available in order to demonstrate knowledge in a hands-on, practical manner. The teacher whose profile is represented in Exhibit 3.27 wants time to organize, the opportunity to use specifics, and the opportunity to use her own ideas.

Evidence of interactive scores also appears in the following student examples. The first student needs a plan and needs to have questions answered correctly. The length of the student's answers is also influenced by his degree of precision. With an "I Use First" level of sequence and precision, this learner is going to follow the typical expectations of school: receive homework, follow directions, use correct information, and write the answers down. The influence of the technical score is also found in his written responses as he states his need to have time to relax after school and in his mention of speaking one-on-one to show what he knows. However, the dominance of the sequential score appears again in the last writ-

---

The Interaction of Sequence, Precision, and Technical

33   26   24   20

F. W. (a student)

What is frustrating?

Assignments frustrate me because the teachers make us write all the time. They don't give us the time to relax after school.

How would you show what you know?

I want the teacher to ask questions and ask us to answer them. Maybe the teachers can make up quizzes and see how much we have learned after studying.

How would you teach others?

I would give the students a week to study and then ask each one questions to see how much they have learned.

Exhibit 3.28

ten response when the student makes it clear he needs sufficient time to study prior to being tested.

Listening to the interaction of the patterns allows the teacher to understand the priority given to each pattern within the learner and to recognize the potential that the learner has to develop a large number of learning strategies by which to complete assignments.

As one student (Sequence, 32; Precise, 29; Technical, 23; and Confluence, 25) explained, "I would do my work well and when she asks questions I'd put my hand up to answer them if I know them. I would show what I know by studying and looking up information. I would ask questions and make charts of the topics that we are doing." This is clearly in keeping with the "I Use First" scores of sequence and precision. However, that is not all the student has to express. She continues,

> Assignments make me frustrated because you always have to write and think and there never is anything fun. Sometimes they are too long, and they make me frustrated. They also give us too much homework so we never have time for ourself. I would make games out of the lessons so they would learn more and so they could enjoy themselves.

The Interaction of Sequence, Precision, Technical, and Confluent

24   21   22   24

I. B. (a student)

What is frustrating?

I like to work together but not like when one goes home and does one thing and another does something else, and we don't meet up.

How would you show what you know?

I would like a small test like a quiz.

How would you teach others?

I would obviously have normal lessons but more outings and group work.

Exhibit 3.29

Within these words, we hear the technical and confluent voice of the learner who "Uses These As Needed." To maintain a positive outlook on learning, it would be helpful to this student if the learning environment in which she finds herself would also address these two patterns.

It is easy to identify within these examples the effects of the mixture of the patterns upon the learner's perspective on school. In some instances, although not common, an individual bridges several of the patterns not using any one first nor avoiding any. The following is an example of this type of interactive pattern.

Notice how the moderate range of the patterns provides a tone of voice that modulates each pattern (small test and quizzes vs. exams; normal lessons, not unusual lessons but with more outings). What a contrast between this voice and the voice of the strong-willed learner.

The Voice That Challenges

There are those learners whose combination of patterns makes them strong-willed learners. This is the case when three of their patterns are in the "I Use This First" category. These learners are often the voice that challenges classmates as well as the teacher. They are perceived as opinionated, stubborn, and always having to be right! They don't work well with other students because their learning combination makes it possible for them to be their own team. The following examples "speak" for themselves.

M. M.'s scores are Sequential, 32; Precise, 34; Technical, 27; and Confluent, 30. She writes very sequentially and very precisely when detailing what frustrates her, how she would show what she knows, and how she would teach:

What frustrates you about assignments?

The thing that frustrates me about assignments is the thing that I arrive home at 3:45, I eat and I start my homework at 4:15. Before 4:30-8:00 I never finish. I never have time to watch TV or to go out, then we have to study for the exams. We shouldn't spend all that time on homework. They never give us enough time to do the projects. We have to do everything at home!

How would you show what you know?

I would suggest that we should do, for example: after ten new lessons of geography the teacher does one or two lessons on revision and asks us some questions like a quiz. We shouldn't stay revising for tests, it's too frustrating. I think we should do what I said above (about quizzes) because it is more fun and less tiring.

If you were the teacher, how would you help students learn?

If I were the teacher I wouldn't have people reading in class without sense because you never understand anything or you forget everything. I would do more outings and more plays and games. More discussions, less homework; quizzes and stuff that the children have fun doing because if they like that, they will look forward to the lesson and have fun and remember what we did!

A. Z., on the other hand, is a strong-willed learner with a different set of interactive patterns. His voice is perfunctory even though he is highly precise. Ten years after completing public schools, this strong-willed learner looks back upon school as a necessary evil that got in the way of his learning. Writing spy novels at age 15, he found his time in school boring and, for the most part, irrelevant to what he wanted to do with his life. His LCI scores of Sequential, 21; Precise, 30; Technical, 26; and Confluent, 32 explain what he relates about school and learning:

What frustrates you about assignments?

They're assigned.

How would you show what you know?

Give a multimedia presentation.

What is your most memorable learning experience in school?

Reading underneath my desk when I should have been doing something boring and assigned.

Not all of the answers we've read are answers we want to hear. Yet the LCI was not developed to mute or censor the voice of the learner. Its intent is to provide a valid and reliable means for people to identify and substantiate the patterns that they use to make sense of learning. Whether a student, a laborer, or a professional, a 6-year-old or a 20-year-old student, the patterns expressed on these pages are the voices of learners. Each is unique, each is articulate, each is worthy of being heard.

Verifying the LCI Scale Scores: Is That Really the Student-Learner I Know?

Even after doing the initial matching of scale scores to written responses, it is important to ask, "Is this the student I see in my class each day?" After all, the strength of any instrument is its accuracy. Making the learner fit the scores isn't the answer. The scores and written responses should amplify the learner's voice, not create a falsetto or stage voice!

If there is one thing we have learned over our years of using the LCI, it is that relying on just our own observations is not sufficient. Although it is true that we have usually observed the learner's use of his or her most dominant processing pattern or patterns, it is most likely that we have missed or misinterpreted the learner's avoidance of certain patterns or on-again, off-again use of those patterns that they "Use as Needed." For example, there are many times when we teachers think that patterns need to be used now and the student apparently does not! So, it is vital that we verify each scale score and the degree to which the learner uses it.

It is also vital to identify any "Teacher-Pleazin'" or "Parent-Pleazin'" responses. This is very important because students who have been told for years that they need to behave in a certain way respond with what they feel is expected. For example, "You need to be more organized! You need to follow directions" and so on. Now, given the opportunity to describe themselves through the LCI, they choose answers that will make them appear to be using these patterns, when in fact, they actually "Avoid" them or "Use Them Only When Needed."

Joey, a highly unorganized, confluent 8-year-old, is a case in point. We know that Joey (Sequential, 26; Precise, 23; Technical, 15; Confluent, 26) isn't anywhere near as sequential as his score would suggest. Even though his score in Sequential is in the high range of "I Use First," it is clear that he is nowhere near as sequential when his work is placed next to someone

Exhibit 3.30

who truly is. Compare his placemat to Erin's, a learner whose scale scores are Sequential, 27; Precise, 20; Technical, 18; Confluent, 22.

Observe the symmetrical little hearts placed methodically on her placemat. If we were to look at her written work, we would see how neat it is compared to the young man who wants to think of himself as sequential. Her notebook is neat and organized, reflective of her Sequential score of 27. Joey's notebook, on the other hand, has pages torn away from the ring binders. Nothing is organized, and nothing is in its correct place. It is a mess. What his placemat does confirm is his high degree of confluence and his modest degree of precision. Joey is picturing a "brain" replacement operation. He uses few words but vivid colors and an impressionistic representation of the operation. His level of precision and his true level of sequence were not enough to prod him into double-checking his spelling. He hastily wrote the word "think" and did not take time to recheck. So, although Joey does not begin his learning with sequence or precision, his message is still very clear and vividly represented in his own unique manner.

Listening for the Accuracy

The results of the LCI are only as accurate as the responses given and the interpretation provided. Therefore, the process of verifying the scale scores requires at the very least a "Use as Needed" degree of sequence.

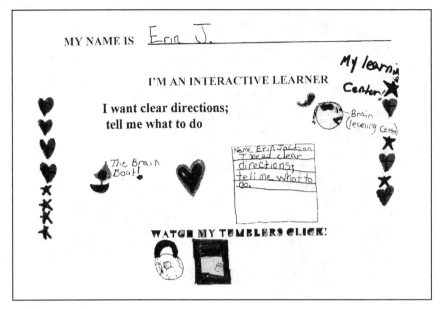

Exhibit 3.31

There are five steps to the verification process, and each needs to be followed carefully.

First, look at the four scores and ask, "Is there variability among these scores?" In other words, do the scores have a degree of variance among them, or do they represent someone who answered all of the items using a 3 (*Sometimes*), resulting in scores of Sequential, 21; Precise, 21; Technical, 21; Confluent, 21? If there is variability, we can assume that the person completing the LCI understood the items and carefully selected an accurate answer among the discrete categories of the continuum. If there is no variability, the instrument needs to be readministered.

Second, we need to check the consistency of the student's responses. If there is inconsistency within the answers, the learner may not have understood the item or may have simply filled in the answers randomly without giving thought to the responses.

Keep in mind that a respondent may consistently answer one subpattern as *Always* and another subpattern totally differently. An example here would be the student who answers the "directions" questions of the sequential pattern as *Always* but the "Neatness, Organized" questions as *Sometimes* or *Almost Never.* What the teacher experiences with this student is someone who asks to have directions repeated several times. This student needs to know if he or she is doing things as the teacher expected. However, this same student's assignments are frequently left at home, on the bus, or under a pile of papers stuffed in his or her desk. Verifying the

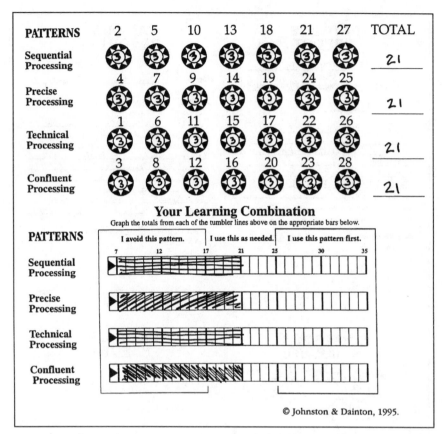

Exhibit 3.32

internal consistency of the subpatterns of each major processing pattern is key to understanding the "total" learner!

Third, we verify the scale scores by anticipating what we will find when we turn the score sheet over and read the respondent's written answers. We can expect that the "I Use This First" pattern or even "I Avoid" pattern will find voice on the page where the student has had an opportunity to put into his or her own words. Here, by using a set of well-established statements gathered from students who "Use First" or "Avoid" certain patterns, we are able to verify at least one or more of the scale scores.

The fourth means of verifying the student's scale scores is to look at samples of the student's work product (see Exhibit 3.33). Here, the teacher can find evidence of strong organization (lists, outlines, neat covers, symmetry in the art work adorning the folders, etc.) or recall the times when the learner asked for more detailed information. Simple artifacts of schoolwork may tell the tale just as well.

PATROL'S REPORT

Name: Anthony Hunter

Grade: 2   Teacher: Mrs. Jewell

Date: 2/6/97

1. Throwing things

2. Going under the seats

3. Yelling on the bus

Patrol's name: Eric Reed
Bus #: 13

PATROL'S REPORT

Name: Dustin Dow

Grade: 4   Teacher: Mrs. Miller

Dustin was singing a Cus word. I told him to please stop because there were little kids on the bus Then he said my life was a piece of Shit! Then I asked him what he said and he called me

Patrol's name: Samantha
Bus #: 9

a fagit. Then I told him he was reported. When I got off the bus he gave me the finger

PATROL'S REPORT

Name: Elyj. Escobea

Grade: 3   Teacher: Mrs. O'Brian

Date: 2/7/97

It was Not listeing and I gave him 2 warnings

Patrol's name: Marcella
Bus #:

PATROL'S REPORT

Name: Andre Hall

Grade: 4   Teacher: Mrs. Miller

1. Screaming on the bus

2. Switching seats

3. Running in the atutorium

Patrol's name: Caitlin Currie
Bus #: 75

Exhibit 3.33

Finding Other Sounding Boards

Communicate With Others

While your evidence in support of the validity of the student's LCI scores continues to grow, there is still more that can be done. Seek external verification of their scores. Talk to the student's former teachers, parents, coaches, or guidance counselor. A simple form can assist you in doing this (see Exhibit 3.34).

Talk to the Learner

Finally, and most importantly, the confirmation of the combination of patterns needs to come from the student's mouth. Sit down and talk to the student about the LCI scores. Begin the dialogue about learning. Delve for details, if appropriate; never challenge, make light of, or demean any pattern. And never, ever refer to any score as a weakness! After all, this is who the learner is, and it is this combination that the learner can use to energize himself or herself to be a strong, engaged, and successful learner.

The interpretation of scores is a vital step to beginning an understanding of the learner and identifying a place to begin to talk and listen to the learner about learning.

What to Do After Administering the LCI?

Begin this phase of listening to the voice of the learner by engaging all students in the discovery of their learning voices. Build a classroom graph or a group chart using the descriptive phrases to emphasize the combination of scores.

To help learners become more aware of their patterns, videotape the students working on a project. Look for the patterns in action! Rewind, replay, and discuss what you see. Talk about what was going on inside their heads as they worked with others within their group. Do the ideal vacation; or the ideal gift—where the learner could use his or her unique learning patterns, draw a name from a hat, talk to the person about his or her learning patterns, and then design the ideal gift for that person.

With older students, after completing the above activities, move on to teaching the conscious use of patterns through "Freeze action" assignments and "Freeze action" projects. At critical points, call out "Freeze." Have the students record what they were thinking, doing, and feeling. Have them analyze this in light of their unique learning combinations. What patterns were they using, avoiding, or deciding that they would

Directions: Please make a check before the statements that you observe about _____. Thank you for your cooperation.

(Learner's Name) _____

_____ becomes frustrated when the directions aren't clear or don't make sense.

_____ doesn't work well when he/she doesn't have good instructions.

_____ hates it when the directions are changed in the middle of an assignment.

_____ finds it hard when the assignment isn't organized or isn't explained thoroughly.

_____ wants you to go over and over the assignment until he/she understands it.

_____ likes you to go slowly and make sure everyone is at the same spot.

_____ likes to practice answers by going over and over them.

_____ likes to have time to study and to complete work in class.

_____ gets upset when more than one assignment is given and no time is given to do the work and go over it in class.

_____ gets upset when he/she doesn't have enough time to do a thorough job.

_____ wants time to make his/her work look neat and to make sure his/her answers are correct.

_____ wants to know all the answers and what will be on the test.

_____ wants you to see that his/her work is correct.

_____ gets upset when he/she doesn't know all the answers because he/she likes doing the work right so that he/she gets a good grade.

_____ gets upset when there isn't enough information or can't find the information and the answers aren't in the book.

_____ gets upset when you don't go into detail and explain things.

_____ takes notes and likes to do activities to reinforce the information presented.

_____ likes trivia.

_____ likes to show people that he/she knows by answering questions.

_____ likes to take tests.

Exhibit 3.34 Teacher External Verification List

_____ likes to write rather than speak publicly.

_____ wants hands-on activities that interest him instead of taking notes, doing book work, or writing about it.

_____ wants the tools to demonstrate knowledge hands-on.

_____ wants to build things.

_____ wants a real challenging project with a point to it and time to figure it out.

_____ needs to run around outside.

_____ needs more breaks during the day.

_____ doesn't let you know what he/she knows.

_____ wants to work alone.

_____ wants real-life experiences.

_____ wants to do the topic that is being learned about.

_____ gets upset when required to follow the teacher's ideas.

_____ gets upset when not allowed to use own ideas.

_____ doesn't like to do an assignment in one certain way.

_____ doesn't like following lots of rules and regulations.

_____ likes to use imagination.

_____ likes to explore new things.

_____ likes to work with people who are curious and don't do assignments in just one way.

_____ likes learning in a creative, fun, entertaining way.

_____ likes coming up with artistic and crafty things.

_____ likes to do storytelling using pictures and imagination.

_____ likes to write the way he/she talks.

_____ likes writing stories using his/her own ideas.

_____ likes to do skits and dress-up like historic persons.

_____ likes to stand up and talk.

Exhibit 3.34 Continued

need to use? Repeat this exercise using learner coaches to talk the student through the place in the assignment where he or she became lost or frustrated. Model this for the class. Videotape two students doing this. Play it for the class and discuss it.

Listen and Learn

Once you have reviewed the makeup of each pattern and discussed the learning combinations that they form, it is time to move to the next step in the LCI process—discussing how to use the student's learning combination in a manner that unlocks his or her will to strive to achieve an array of learning goals. This means that you need to listen, and the learner needs the opportunity to talk. This is where the learner begins to unlock the will to learn; this is where the teacher begins to understand how to facilitate this process.

As Mark Micallef described, "The Learning Combination Inventory identifies what comprises your learning cleverness. We are all clever in some way. That's the key. We only need to know that about ourselves." The LCI identifies the voice and the message of the voice, and then it amplifies the message, converting the patterns into the learner's own expressions.

Once we've begun to hear the voice of the learner in our classroom, we can no longer ignore it. It is a lyric, a melody, a beat, a tune that keeps going around and around in our heads. Our learners' voices and their messages about learning help to make sense out of what we have been hearing, seeing, and possibly mistaking as classroom noise and distraction. Now we know it's the voice of the learner, and we have a valid means of identifying and beginning the work of nurturing, supporting, and facilitating its growth.

And This Is What They Said

I have come across other learning-style theories, such as the Dunn and Dunn and 4MAT, but the LCI is the most practical and easiest to use. It is more down-to-earth, teacher, parent, and even student friendly. Moreover, it takes into consideration multiple intelligences as well as emotional intelligence.

MARLENE GUTIERREZ
Secondary Science Teacher
Manila, Philippines

Note

1. People who granted permission for use of their LCI score sheets are Sarah Berninger; Gregg Carbaugh; Burt Diamond; Samuel Feinstein, DDS; Jo Anne Glass; Rose Gutenkunst; Jerry Haag, MD; Herman James; Valla Klettke; Mark A. Micallef; Daniel Price; Reuben Singelton; Kay

Stahlberger; Linda Wittmann; and Doreen Gatt Coleiro from Malta. In addition, more than 60% of the examples used in this chapter were derived from LCIs administered in Malta. The fact that these responses are identical to those of students in the United States, Northern Ireland, and England provides evidence of the universal voice of the learner and the power of the LCI to capture that voice.

References and Selected Bibliography

Addy, L. (1996, April). *Challenging the assumptions: The motivation and learning of children who have developmental coordination disorder.* Paper presented at the annual meeting of the American Educational Research Association, New York.

Curry, L. (1990). A critique of the research on learning styles. *Educational Leadership, 48*(2), 50-56.

Eisner, E. (1997). Cognition and representation: A way to pursue the American dream? *Phi Delta Kappan, 78*(5), 349-360.

Hayes, M. (1996, April). *Finding the voice: Hearing the voice—the underrepresented in the reform movement.* Paper presented at the American Educational Research Association's annual meeting, New York.

Johnston, C. (1997). *Many voices—one message: A cross-cultural study of student learning processes with implications for learners, teachers, and reformers.* Paper presented at the European Institute on Research on Learning and Instruction Symposium, Athens, Greece.

Johnston, C. (1997). *Unlocking the will to learn: Teachers and students as partners.* Paper presented to the annual conference of the British Educational Research Association, York, England.

Johnston, C., & Dainton, G. (1997). *The learning combination inventory (Manual).* Thousand Oaks, CA: Corwin.

Johnston, C., & Dainton, G. (1997). *The learning combination inventory (Professional Form).* Thousand Oaks, CA: Corwin.

Johnston, J. (1996). *A study of student learning processes with implications for learners, teachers and reformers. Will the real learner raise a hand?* Paper presented at the annual meeting of the American Educational Research Association, New York.

Keefe, J., & Ferrell, B. (1990). Developing a defensible learning style paradigm. *Educational Leadership, 48*(2), 57-61.

Mifsud, J. (1996). *Listening to the learner: Harnessing learner characteristics to shape school reform.* Paper presented at the American Educational Research Association's annual meeting, New York.

Snow, R., & Jackson, D. (1992). *Assessment of conative constructs for educational research and evaluation: A catalogue.* Washington, DC: U.S. Department of Education, Office of Educational Research and Improvement.

Further Reading

Johnston, C. (1997). *Institutional research and planning.* Rowan University Research Briefs, March 1997 [On-line]. Available: http://www. letmelearn.org

To most teachers, as well as parents, the slow learning child is a complete enigma. One day he learns the classroom material to perfection; the next he seems to have forgotten every bit of it. In one activity he excels all the other children; in the next he performs like a two-year-old. Too often these aberrant performances are attributed to willful misbehavior, stupidity or lack of interest. Actually in many cases, the child's problems are not his fault. His central nervous system processes information in a little different way than that of other children.

Kephart, 1960, introduction

4

When Sounds of Silence
Are All You Hear

This chapter is about Mark and Company. The reader may already know Mark and his counterparts, the students who sit off to the side of the room by themselves. Angry, aloof, and always with a countenance that communicates the single question, "How much longer can this go on?"

Hearing Mark's Voice

Mark is the learner whose voice is silent and whose message is loud and clear: "I can figure out, solve, build, and fix just about anything, except school!" This message within the learner begins early as a quietly intoned question: "Why can't I make school work for me?" It reaches a crescendo by the middle school years in the percussive declaration, "I don't care if I can make school work!"

This book began by encouraging the reader to listen to the voice of the learner and understand the message. From its foreword through each of the chapters, the message is the same: The voice of the learner is the best source we have for guiding effective teaching and successful learning.

Now, in Chapter 4, we come to the real conscience of this text, to the very heart of our listening—listening to the learner whose message we don't understand because it is foreign to us as teachers. The content of this chapter challenges what we value as learners and what we perpetuate as teachers under the guise of successful instruction. This chapter introduces us to the voice of silence and the message of frustration, and in doing so, it confronts us with our worst fear—failure.

AUTHOR'S NOTE: Individuals who contributed case studies for use in this chapter are Michael Buccialia, Sandra Dorrel, Daniel Greenspan, Laura Hammond, Mardi Lesher, Helen McCracken, Kathy McHale, and Monica Wells.

Meeting Up With Mark

I first met Mark as a feisty 6-year-old in an urban district. I met him in Malta, too, when he was in 8th grade. I found Mark in an upper-middle-class suburban high school on the East Coast. He was 15, classified by the Child Study Team as Perceptually Impaired, by other students as a loser, and by his teachers as "just putting in time." I've met Mark's grandmother in Palo Alto, California; his parents in New Jersey; and his disciplinarian in Belfast, Northern Ireland. Mark was my graduate assistant one year. I have also met Mark at Rotary International. Mark does get around!

Mark has many faces, many ages, many stages, and many locales, but the profile is the same. He is

- Capable
- Underachieving
- Unmotivated
- Not working up to potential while in school
- Highly engaged in learning outside of school—learning about how to make the world work
- Involved in finding solutions to real problems

Frequently, Mark and Company are high achievers as adults who look back on their school years with bewilderment and at their success out in the real world with pride. These are individuals who begin learning by using the pattern of Technical Reasoning and complement this with a mixture of varying degrees of the Sequential, Precise, and Confluent patterns.

Mark Is a Member of My Family

I have a Mark in my family. Her name is Emily. She doesn't sit in her seat. She kneels in her chair. She wants to be up and out of her seat moving, touching, getting into things. She's my granddaughter. She began building with Lincoln Logs when she was 3 years old. Sophisticated buildings; everything comes apart; everything has to be examined for its use, its purpose, and how it works. And she constantly reminds me of who she is first and foremost as a learner:

November 13, 1997

It is the day before Emily's fifth birthday. This morning, as I was frosting cupcakes for her to take to school, I found myself saying, "Emily, no. You can't help me frost these." "No, Emily, you can't play with the butter knife. You'll get frosting all over your clothes." "Emily, please put the colored sugars down." Finally, I spied her with her hands in the silverware drawer, just rattling the spoons and fiddling with the utensil tray. The drawer was just barely open, but she had slid her hands into it. I said with exasperation, "For crying out loud, Emily, get your hands out of that drawer. Who wants to eat off those after you have had your hands all over them?" Emily quietly disappeared into the living room. I found her there sitting on the edge of the couch.

Regretting my sharp comment, I put my arm around her and asked, "Emily, what was going through your mind when you decided to put your hands in the drawer?" Emily slowly raised her head and in her most sincere voice simply stated, "Grandma, I just needed to put my hands on something."

Christine Johnston
Personal journal

For Emily, the tools of learning begin with her use of real tools. Here is a classic example of the conative voice of learning: "observable but not the most articulate. It is a drumbeat, a Morse code, a tapping of the pencil, a scraping of the desk, a staring out the window," a playing with the silverware, "an action-oriented means of communication—the choreography of learning rather than the lyrics. The message is loud and clear, and even though the voice is different, the communication is audible to the trained listener." Even though I write books about the topic, I, too, forget to apply what I know within my own family context!

At age five, Emily has been labeled by her teacher as "inattentive." Her teacher described a student who "can't sit in her seat, and goes off by herself and plays." Already the words "hyperactivity and attention deficit" have been spoken by the teacher—this about a child who will spend hours working with Legos and Play Mobile toys, puzzles, Lincoln Logs, or on the trail of an elusive spider or a rock that needs to be found!

Getting the Message

The learners about whom this chapter is written have a set of interactive learning patterns that is dominated by the Technical Reasoning pattern. Their learning combination is most influenced by technical reasoning, followed by, or in concert with, their use of sequence, precision, and confluence. Obviously, the degree to which they use these also influences their overall learning combination. However, whatever the combination, it is the fact that they begin their learning through the use of their technical reasoning that not only sets them apart from, but sets them outside of, the standards of paper-and-pencil-driven learning. Unlike those who use sequential and precise to survive schooling, the learner who begins a task with technical reasoning finds that this approach creates a barrier rather than a bridge within the classroom.

Compared to Other Learners

When compared to other learners, the child whose learning combination is dominated with technical reasoning appears less academic, less in tune with the paper-and-pencil world of schooling. A 3-year study that followed 42 children from their first through third years of school suggests that children with learning combinations that are dominated by the use of technical reasoning are more likely to be off grade level or referred to the Child Study Team than are students who begin their learning using their sequential or precise patterns. The examples that follow illustrate the effects of traditional schooling upon this type of learner.

The Voices of Two
Very Different Learners

A comparison of Samantha and Mark provides a clear example of the difference in the voices of learners. Samantha would be termed the "ideal student." When she was administered the LCI early in her Grade 1 year, she amazed the person who was administering the Inventory by announcing that "nothing" frustrates her about learning. She was emphatic when she stated that "I have a system. I use it and my teacher likes it." The administrator noted in the margin of the Inventory that Samantha presented herself with great confidence. She seated herself primly at her desk, smoothed out her dress, folded her hands, and announced that she was ready. Samantha's 3 years of consistently high scores in sequential and precise processing indicate her "fit" with schooling and the traditional school learning environment. She needs consistency, patterns, rules, and structure. Her answers indicate that she responds well to a classroom in which these are used foremost.

Mark's scores, on the other hand, indicate what happens when a learner is unable to take on the behaviors of the student as deemed necessary for promotion and success. Mark's scores over time change as he comes to grips with his educational environment.

The evolution of Mark's learning processes within a formal school environment are captured in the change over time of his LCI scale scores and his written responses to the three open-ended questions. The reader sees his change from the ideal student ready to take in and remember lots

Samantha

Grade 1	Grade 2	Grade 3
Scores: 27-25-13-19	Scores: 27-26-11-20	Scores: 29-27-13-19
What frustrates you about learning?	**What frustrates you about learning?**	**What frustrates you about learning?**
Nothing. I have a system. I use it and my teacher likes it.	*When the teacher changes the directions.*	When I don't have time to recopy my work.
How would you like to show what you know?	**How would you like to show what you know?**	**How would you like to show what you know?**
Do spelling.	*Answer lots of questions.*	Take a spelling test.
What would make learning fun for you?	**How would you teach others?**	**How would you teach others?**
I like school.	*I would teach just like Mrs. B.*	I would say sit down and listen. Do your work carefully.

Exhibit 4.1

of information in an organized manner to the real Mark-as-learner, a child who uses technical reasoning and confluence (action and risk taking) to make learning work for him. However, Mark was never the "ideal" student. He entered school with the belief that he should know lots of information and do lots of worksheets. It is only after he is in school that he recognizes that this is not how he learns. Thus begins the conflict between schooling and learning until, by his second year, he openly questions the entire "school" routine. His initial scores reflect his beliefs about what he should respond if he is a good student.

In subsequent years, his scores reflect Mark-the-learner. The following description of Mark as a learner and as a student, provided by his guidance counselor, gives further validation of the evolving learning profile recorded over the 3-year period.

> *This child became a part of my caseload in 1st grade because of his difficulties in the classroom. He would not follow directions; he would frequently be sent to my office.*

Mark

Grade 1	Grade 2	Grade 3
Scores: 35-31-19-15	Scores: 27-15-31-27	Scores: 19-07-35-27

What frustrates you about learning?	**What frustrates you about learning?**	**What frustrates you about learning?**
When I only know a little bit about what the teacher is teaching.	*The things we do in class are weird.*	*It's nothing but asering cwestons.*

How would you like to show what you know?	**How would you like to show what you know?**	**How would you like to show what you know?**
Give me lots of papers to do.	*I wood do a page in a journal.*	*I wood show how I play Mines Plus.*

What would make learning fun for you?	**How would you teach others?**	**How would you teach others?**
Learning about bicycle parts.	*I would teach them about the subject.*	*I would teach them by playing games.*

Exhibit 4.2

This child is one who spent a great deal of his second-grade time in my office, sent there because he was not producing, or he was touching someone or something he should not be touching, or he was physically someplace where he should not be.

He is now in the third grade. These are some of the comments his teacher has given me permission to relate. First, this individual now sits right next to his teacher. She feels he does not feel he can be successful in the classroom if he is sitting with other students. He needs to be completely by himself. He also will just look around. He is not malicious with it. He doesn't understand that he is disruptive. He will sing when he is working. He taps his pencil. She laments that there is no computer in her classroom because when he gets the opportunity to work hands-on, he thrives. The way she has found success for him this year is to grade all of his manipulative tasks and arranges a situation whereby whenever he has a paper-and-pencil or school task to do, he can do those in small spurts. "It has been a constant negotiation, and nothing is ever easy."

> *Her response to my question, "What kind of program do you think*
> *this child could be successful in?" was, "It would have to be a vocational*
> *thing. The way school is set up now, there is no school on our level where*
> *he can be successful." But she feels that there are some classrooms where*
> *he can be more successful than in others. Behavior-wise, he has a lot of*
> *problems. When he leaves my classroom, he goes into a highly struc-*
> *tured environment, and he finds it impossible to sit and not move. That*
> *will frequently get him into trouble.*
>
>

Mardi Lesher
personal interview

Mark is a classic example of the learner who finds it difficult, if not impossible, to use his learning processes within a highly sequential and precise, orderly, and controlled learning environment. Mark begins with the best intentions informed by the messages of both parents and teachers: "Pay attention. Listen to the teacher. Learn what the teacher is teaching." These are the behaviors that are required, expected, and valued. Only when he is with a teacher who understands his struggles to conform is he able to use his learning processes in any type of an effective manner.

To understand what the future holds for Mark, we need only fast-forward the school years and look at Dan. I first became acquainted with Dan through my university's academic computing office. Dan made my computer run and run well. So when I read, "Lover of science reaps reward for being eternally curious: He's going to Hawaii this week to help NASA study the Hale-Bopp comet" and saw Dan's photo, I was intrigued and read on—and I discovered Mark-the-learner in Dan-the-scientist. What follows is Dan's story in his own words.

Dan-the-Learner

Again and again, even in college and now, the way the educational system works has not been very helpful to me. It's been the things outside of it that have been good for me. I just saw school as this horrible concentration camp. I didn't learn much in school, but I would spend all my free time learning on my own. That's what made me feel good.

My teachers always said I wasn't paying attention in class. I wasn't paying attention because they were boring me! So they [the teachers] would call my parents and tell them I wasn't doing well, that I wasn't doing my homework, which I wasn't. No one tried to sit down and ask me why I wasn't doing my homework. I didn't do it because I didn't want to. I hated it. I hated school. I hated going every day. Nobody ever asked me what I did in my free time. Nobody ever asked me, "What do you read?" And so as I got into the 6th and 7th grade, they labeled me an underachiever.

Dan

College Senior
Scores: 27-30-33-30

What frustrates you about learning?

There is a lot of frustration in knowing that I must only regurgitate what I am supposed to—while not really getting a chance to show what I really learned (I prefer essay to multiple choice).

How would you like to show what you know?

I would write an essay, build a project, or give a speech on the subject or have an extended discussion, a Q/A session with the instructor.

How would you teach others?

By getting them involved and trying to find a reason (for them) that they would care or want to know. My feeling is that conceptualization should come before technical skills. Also, it is critical to pay attention to each individual's emotional state, and not to judge all by one metric. The Hell with A-F; does the person know something?

Exhibit 4.3

They'd say, "Your tests are so high, but you're not performing in class." And so then this dichotomy developed where I was in the advanced placement classes and the remedial classes in the same semester. Maybe I'd be in advanced placement in reading, but I'd be in remedial math. And nobody thought this was strange. And if they did, nobody did anything about it.

I had a terrible time with math. I had very high math anxiety. I found a book written by a man in 1905, and the opening chapter said something like, "All that time you've spent in class, reciting your multiplication tables, is a complete waste of your time." And I thought, thank God, somebody else feels that way. I finally learned to love math because I love physics, and I love electronics.

I remember the first time I tried something. I wanted to know about this magic that happened when I turned a switch on and the light would come on. So I got a switch, a light socket, and some wire. I put it together, pulled the switch, and it blew up. So I tried to figure out what I had done wrong. I put it back together, and I tried it the second time, and it worked.

I did this kind of thing all the time until I realized I couldn't keep reinventing the wheel. That's when I learned that the beauty about math is it allows you to figure out something is going to be right before you blow something up. I learned from reading about the people who had done it, and I recognized that the real achievement had not been in doing something, but in understanding it. And the tool for that was mathematics. I knew then that if I didn't begin to learn and understand the math, I'd never begin to reach that goal I wanted. So I began to understand the use and the beauty of mathematics before I started understanding how to do it. To me the most important thing is why something is important to know. Then tell me how to do it.

In the middle of my junior year in high school, I stopped going. I found an alternative school that gave us a lot of free time to go find out things. I went around to different universities and asked heads of cardiology departments if I could be a part of their research programs. For two and a half years, I studied medicine, particularly cardiology. I attended two unit surgeries; I built electronic devices to help probe animal blood patterns. I really did graduate-level work from the ages of $16\frac{1}{2}$ to 18.

I have felt like a failure my whole life. I mean who wants to go through school feeling you're already losing? I certainly understand why the highest suicide rate is among high schoolers.

I wonder how many people there are just like me who are wandering around feeling like a loser. I remember when working at NASA, I had this dream where I would come back and give presentations and show really cool things I did and get students all excited, and then explain that I couldn't add fractions until after I graduated from high school. I was labeled an underachiever in school. I failed in school, but I still got the chance to work with NASA on this project. On the trip to Hawaii for NASA, I met one of the world's foremost geophysicists, and he told me he couldn't add fractions until he was 23. This guy has PhDs from all over the world, and he told me that! And it was so cool because he was just like me.

The Tale of Technical Learners

Mark and Company literally involves a cast of thousands. Cited in this chapter are only a few of the cases that typify the nature of this learning combination and the response of schooling to it. The response begins young. Billy, age 6, is a case in point. His scale scores, as well as his written responses, indicate his learning combination consists of an "I Avoid" level of sequence and an "I Use First" level of technical reasoning. These, coupled with a low range of "I Use as Needed" confluence, suggest that he is likely to be misunderstood as a learner and is unlikely to risk attempting to explain himself to his teacher.

Billy, Yet Another Generation of Dan

Billy's teacher's profile of him clearly suggests that he is not producing acceptable "schooling" results. For the purpose of emphasis here, I have taken the liberty of dividing the teacher's comments into two categories: schooling comments and learning comments.

Schooling Comments

> *Billy has a short attention span and does become distracted easily. Billy is also disorganized. He is having trouble learning math concepts, and he needs to build his sight vocabulary. He doesn't seem to take school too seriously. Billy may have some learning disabilities and should be tested for this soon. He has been referred to the Child Study Team.*

Learning Comments

> *Billy is a very unique young boy. He is a very technical student. When the class works on a project that involves building, he excels. His project is usually three-dimensional, whereas the rest may be one-dimensional. He tends to be stubborn with his ideas and has a hard time grasping new concepts. He believes his ideas are correct, and we just don't understand. He asks a lot of questions, but his questions don't really relate to the topic.*
>
> *When working on making Christmas decorations, Billy and his table partner had an argument about the red paint. Rshad told him the paint was dried up and couldn't be used. Billy didn't accept that answer. He kept working with the paint until he was able to get it to work. He was right! He has real stick-to-itiveness.*

There is a real contradiction between these two summaries: Billy is easily distracted versus Billy has real stick-to-itiveness. At one point, Billy's stick-to-itiveness is seen as stubbornness, and at another, as the positive trait of persistence. Art Costa refers to the characteristic of persistence as a sign of intelligent behavior. Other aspects of Billy's learning profile are explained by his LCI scores: Billy's lack of interest in reading and sight vocabulary are explained by his low score in precise and his high score in technical reasoning. It is the latter pattern that makes it difficult for the learner to value "book" learning within the confines of school. Billy's disorganization is explained by his avoidance of the use of sequence. His abilities to build and to solve problems are commendable learning traits attributable to his high use in technical reasoning.

After reading Billy's profile, we are left with several important questions: Are his behaviors indicative of a child with learning disabilities, or

---

Billy

Grade 1

Scores: 15-21-31-18

What frustrates you about learning?

Directions.

How would you like to show what you know?

Create a filmstrip.

How would you teach others?

Tell them.

Exhibit 4.4

are they indicative of a child who begins learning tasks by using his technical reasoning first? Is his disorganization magnified in the eyes of his teacher, who is significantly more sequential? Will a referral to the Child Study Team preempt opportunities for his teacher to build a teacher-learner relationship that helps Billy develop as a confident learner, or will he assume a "loser" status within his first year of schooling?

Mark and Company—What Does Their Learning Future Hold?

The future of Mark and Company as successful learners is bleak without teachers, classmates, and parents coming to an awareness of the voice of these learners. However, awareness is only the first step. Each teacher and parent needs to take action that will result in the following outcomes for teachers:

- An increase in patience
- A decrease in negative perceptions
- A more open means of communicating with the student
- An expanded teaching repertoire

To accomplish this challenging agenda, teachers need to confront their own biases and prejudices about what is legitimate learning. If a teacher remains convinced that learning always requires the use of words, means knowing the "correct" answers, means focusing on book-fed facts, means mastering the use of paper and pencils, and can only be assessed through tests, then schooling will continue and learning will diminish.

Clearly, we need to reflect upon our own learning combination even as we identify the individual learning combinations of our students. We need to anticipate the type of assignments and learning patterns that are going to bring relevance and action into the classroom.

We need to ask, along with our learners, questions such as, "Does it work?" "Did the solution you came up with fix the situation?" "Did your unorthodox approach open up an entirely new body of knowledge or key insight?" When we ask those types of questions, we begin to reverse the tide of schooling and begin to facilitate successful learning.

Taking the Next Step

As I drafted this section of the manuscript, I sought the counsel of learners who use technical reasoning as their lead learning pattern. I wanted to make certain that I represented the next step accurately, neither over-stating nor understating it. One school administrator who not only uses his technical reasoning "first," but whose son does also, responded with these helpful remarks:

> *You've captured the essence of the technical learner. Just remember that communication is still the biggest issue. The technical person communicates by doing. Consequently, teachers need to be able to interpret actions, things produced, things given to them, or things done for them as that student's form of communication. That student will never sit down and compose a letter of appreciation. To technical students, a note is just words. Words are too impersonal. But if they do something, well, that has more personal value, compared to just words that everybody uses.*
>
> *There is a deep emotional component to the technical pattern that is often overlooked by teachers and parents. They see only a general stoic outward reaction to things. Teachers and parents need to develop skills to be able to recognize these students' "silent voices and silent emotions."*

No Easy Answers

There is no doubt that learners who use technical reasoning suffer at the hands of a system that does not hear their voices. However, the purpose of this text is not only to convey that message but also to suggest how to make things different. Again, if we listen to the learners whose profiles and words have been presented in the earlier pages, we hear the answer:

- Recognize the pattern for what it is, not what it isn't.
- Give personal attention.
- Listen to the learner publicly; respond privately.
- Notice the difference in their learning response to learning over time.
- Offer an encouraging word.
- Respect the tools of learning used within this pattern.

Overcoming the Bias

As a friend and colleague of mine shared with me, "It's really freeing to know who you are as a learner and to celebrate it. But as a teacher, you need to be prepared to know who you are as a learner and walk through the wall that separates you from other learners. You have to go through the wall before you can serve the learner who is different from you."

One of the reasons that we struggle so with accepting other patterns of learning is because they are foreign to us. They are strange. We can't relate to them. They are uncomfortable. They don't communicate the degree or depth of learning to us in the same manner as those patterns that are most familiar to us.

Recently, I received a gift, a fascinating book on foreign affairs, that explains that whenever we are asked to internalize something new, it is as if we are inviting the unknown, the feared, and the unfamiliar into our very being. This insight helps me understand why, once we know about the difference in learning between ourselves and our students, we find it difficult to let down our guard and accept their differing learning patterns. We simply are not at ease allowing those differences in learning to invade our educational territory! These students, through no fault of their own, appear to us to have foreign behaviors and learning voices, making it difficult for us to welcome them into our classroom.

And Mark Begat Dan, and Dan Begat Ben, and Ben Begat . . .

Ben is a classic example of the learner who could "do it all" if he chooses to, but who has allowed his technical reasoning to hold sway. There is a good reason for this. Ben's science intelligence is very strong. This, coupled with his learning pattern, which is led by technical reasoning, makes

---

Ben

Grade 4

Scores: 26-22-33-23

What frustrates you about learning?

She makes me do very long assignments.

How would you like to show what you know?

I would show her by telling her.

How would you teach others?

I would give them derections and tell them to figer it out.

Exhibit 4.5

him a budding Edison, not a candidate for the Pulitzer Prize. A news arti-
cle about Ben ("Annual Shopping Spree," 1997) provides insights into this
learner that would not be found in his school cumulative folder.

> Nine-year-old Ben C. was pleased with his purchase yesterday—a
> vacuum cleaner to add to his collection. Ben carried the vacuum,
> which was almost bigger than he was, as he walked with his fam-
> ily. He paid $8 for the vacuum and said his collection now num-
> bers 25.
>
> Ben didn't elaborate much on his love of vacuums, except to
> say that his oldest is from 1907 and that he likes fixing machines
> and the noise that they make.
>
> If this were all there were to it, we could say, "Interesting," and
> move on. But listen to his mother's description.
>
> You want to know what I have learned about Ben and his
> learning. . . . He is very special I know, but he has to do this stuff
> [school work]! He is very moody and is not happy unless he is
> doing something like creating something. We went to Edmond
> Scientific today, and he was in all his glory. He is now making a
> phone from scratch. For a nine-year-old, he is very advanced. He
> uses the soldering iron and is making the circuit board of a phone.
>
> I am sure Ben's teacher does not understand him. In fact she
> is one very frustrated woman this year. I did have a thought as to
> why Ben is beginning to dislike math. It is just a guess but the
> teacher has the students write the math terms and memorize

definitions in their math journal. Ben must hate that and sees no meaning in it. (p. A1)

Katie's "Declaration of Learning Independence"

Katie represents another type of learner who has been successful because she uses all of her patterns to make school work for her. However, Katie has reached the point where she can no longer muffle the voice of technical reasoning within her, nor muffle the disdain she feels for the schooling she is experiencing.

As a part of an English assignment, Katie was asked to reflect upon who she was as a learner. She had just finished a poetry unit. Katie's written response, rife with sarcasm, follows:

Katie C, Ph.D., M.D., Ed.D., Dpm, MAD

I love to learn. It is so great. I wish I could have school all year around. I think I should go to school for 12 hours a day and do homework for another 6 hours. I like to learn by doing lots of busy work. I also like to build things and tear them down. I love it when things are unorderly, and I hate people that need everything perfectly. I love tests and long reports, especially the Iowa, SAT, and EWT tests. They are so fun. I wish I could do them everyday. I also like to write fictional stories because I can let my imagination run wild. I like to cook things, but I would never eat the food I make because it is lethal.

I hate reading poems especially the ones that take a year to write and are only two lines long. I can't fathom why someone would waste their time on that. I also like studying disease such as scurvy, lockjaw, gangrene, and influenza. I really hate it when people make fun of me. I don't like teachers with no imagination, and I love eating glue and other office supplies.

I am technical and proud of it.

Katie is seething. She sees little relevance to what she is asked to do, and at the midpoint of her eighth year in school, she allows her anger to spill over onto the written page. When asked by her teacher if this was what she wanted to submit as her final draft, Katie responded with a less caustic but no less powerful paragraph:

I am technical, which means I like to learn with my hands. I don't like to write about things, but I like to do experiments. I can't stand not having something to do, and I think I get in the most trouble when I am

---

Katie

Grade 8
Age: 13
Scores: 20-18-34-23

What frustrates you about learning?

When they are dumb (assignments) and I don't like to do them, and I have to write a lot.

How would you like to show what you know?

I would like to do a report, a fun one, not writing about it or taking a test.

How would you teach others?

I'd let them do a lot of fun hands things.

I would not make them read poems.

Exhibit 4.6

> *sitting with nothing to do. I also like to build things, and I don't like to read poems. I wish I could stay home from school and put my time to better use.*

Katie's message is clear: Make it relevant, or let me be at home where I can do meaningful things—really learn away from and apart from school! Katie's case is interesting because her learning combination includes levels of sequence and precision that have served her well during her early years of schooling. But as she reaches adolescence, her high degree of technical reasoning, her desire for independence, and her need for relevance assert themselves, bringing the technical reasoning to the surface. As Katie enters high school, she will remain a real challenge to her teachers, who will identify her as bright and capable, but not motivated to do the work.

There Is Hope for Mark and Company and Katie

I would never have embarked upon this chapter without having in hand examples of how teachers have used their awareness of students' learning combinations to make a difference with the learner who uses the technical reasoning pattern first. What follows is an example of a successful intervention that forms a segue into Chapter 5, a chapter that deals solely with teachers and students who have formed successful learning partnerships based upon the commitment to understand each other as learner and teacher.

Brandon and His Team

The following case involves the perspective of two teachers—a regular education and a special education teacher working as teaching partners within an "inclusion" classroom. The following is a summary of Brandon's progress in fifth grade. This case analysis was developed jointly by Brandon's homeroom and in-class support teachers:

> *Our initial observation was that Brandon "is very unorganized and disheveled." In September, he talked frequently while the lesson was going on and was disruptive during lessons. By "disruptive" we mean he was in and out of his desk, searching for paper in his desk, talking to neighbors, and looking for books. We would stop frequently during lessons to bring him back to task and have him quiet down. When we did give him a task or the teacher was able to work with him one-on-one, he was very motivated and cooperative in his learning.*
>
> *We became very concerned as the days and weeks passed because he was becoming more disruptive and more disorganized, to the point that when you gave him an assignment, his was always lost. We would witness him writing, but when it came to collecting it, Brandon's was never in the pile. We also felt that there was some possible ADHD involved with his disorganizational activities.*
>
> *Brandon had been referred to the Pupil Assistance Committee (PAC) by his fourth-grade teacher. When his name came before the PAC meeting in the fall, it was recommended that Brandon be retained next year because academically he was not performing on grade level.*
>
> *However, after we gave the inventory (LCI) and realized that Brandon loves to do things with his hands (he loves to draw, build, you name it, as long as it's something that he can use his hands on), we took an entirely different approach with him. To start with, we gave him a cup with Fun Tac in it to play with. We were amazed what that did for this child. It kept him centered and occupied, but right with us during lessons. He now was tuned in to what we were doing.*
>
> *As we focused our efforts on Brandon, we realized that he was a child who does have potential. When we put our kids into cooperative learning groups, we were just incredibly in awe of how well he performed in a group. He took over the group as far as leadership went,*

Brandon

Grade 5
Age: 10
Scores: 32-28-35-22

What frustrates you about learning?

Too much work and questings [questions] to do.

How would you like to show what you know?

I would go up to the bord and wright everything I learned on the bord to show her.

How would you teach others?

I would do everything we had to do even all the work.

Exhibit 4.7

actually giving assignments to other members of the group while he did the artwork. His self-confidence was just beaming. You couldn't help but notice that this boy was feeling very good about himself and what he was doing. When we observed him with this group, he was intent on listening to what they were saying about the facts they were finding for their report. He would respond with comments such as, "Oh really, I didn't know they did that . . . well, we'll put that in the picture too." It was like a light bulb was constantly going off inside of him during his whole cooperative learning process. Brandon really opened our eyes to cooperative learning. Focusing on his interaction, we were able to witness how children learn from other children. Just the fact that he took that leadership role amazed us. He now walks around the classroom more sure of himself. It's a real good feeling to see. He talks very openly about his learning—that he's Sequential, Precise, and Technical. He's also aware that he can learn confluence from his peers.

When we had the follow-up Pupil Assistance Committee meeting, we said we're not going to give up on this child, and we are not going to recommend retention. We explained the LCI to the Committee. We said here was a child we felt would greatly benefit by cooperative learning. Our plan is to put him in as many cooperative groups as possible because, as Brandon wrote, "I like working in a group because I can learn from the people in the group." When they were doing their cooperative project, there was no truer statement. So that's Brandon.

That is Brandon, but more importantly, those are Brandon's teachers! Their insights, their decisions, and their commitment provide hope for the future of this learner.

Actions Do Speak Louder

We cannot come to this point in the chapter without remembering a student who sat in our class, silent of voice and defeated in spirit, struggling each day to tolerate the environment of school. Now that we have the message, now that we have gained a new understanding, it is vital that we take action to prevent this continued loss of human potential. Our actions will speak louder than words to these learners. Learning is an interactive enterprise. We need to be up to the challenge of creating an environment in which all learners can thrive and where they can be actively engaged in the hands-on of learning. This change begins with a commitment spurred on by action.

It could begin as simply as the teacher who, after reading Dan's story, e-mailed the following message to him:

> *Dan, I just completed a graduate course entitled "Unlocking the Will to Learn," and the professor shared an article about your experiences in school and a copy of the interview she had with you. It saddened me to hear all the problems you faced within your educational experience.*
>
> *I am a precise/sequential learner and teacher. My toughest students are the technical/confluent learners. Having read your article, I have made a promise to myself that after 23 years in education, I will try to do my best to reach those who, much like yourself, don't fit in the standard mold of what I have considered the typical student.*
>
> *Thank you for sharing this information with us. Let us hope that we will be able to help another child like yourself who has so much to offer to the world!*

Actions do speak louder.

And This Is What They Said

Teachers and parents need to develop skills to be able to recognize these students' "silent voices and silent emotions."

References and Selected Bibliography

Annual shopping spree draws crowds to market. (1997, December 1). *Burlington County (NJ) Times*, p. A1.

Coleman, K. (1997). *Katie C, Ph.D., M.D., Ed.D., Dpm, MAD.* Unpublished manuscript.

Costa, A. (1987). What human beings do when they behave intelligently and how they can become more so. *BC Journal of Special Education, 11*(3), 239-249.

Johnston, C., & Johnston, J. (1997). *Understanding and using the child's will to learn: A longitudinal study.* Paper presented at the European Conference on Educational Research, Frankfurt, Germany.

Kephart, N. C. (1960). *The slow learner in the classroom.* Columbus, OH: Merrill.

Polk, W. (1997). *Neighbors and strangers.* Chicago: University of Chicago Press.

Warner, M. (1997, April 1). Lover of science reaps reward for being eternally curious. *The Philadelphia Inquirer,* p. B4.

Further Reading

Darling-Hammond, L. (1998). Teacher learning that supports student learning. *Educational Leadership, 55*(5), 6-11.

Maeroff, G. (1998). Altered destinies: Making life better for schoolchildren in need. *Phi Delta Kappan, 79,* 424-432.

Instead of talking all the time about what teachers should teach and what students should learn, we should talk about what teachers and students should do. We should be talking about experiences they should be mutually engaged in.

Smith, 1995, p. 590

5

What Do You Mean by "Two-getherness"?

We have learned to work together. I am highly sequential, P.J. is highly precise, Lance is highly technical, and Corey is highly confluent. When we came together as a group, we wanted to use our own patterns. After we were together for a while, we became interested in each others'. We learned from each other too. Now we don't even think about each others' patterns, we just work together as one!

5th-Grade Learner
Ms. Lorraine Pfeffer's Class
Alloway Township Schools
Spring 1997

Making the Connection

The reader has now arrived at the moment of truth. Up to this point, reading about learning has been interesting, intriguing, and most of all, safe. This chapter moves the reader out of the comfort zone of learning about our learning combinations and into the arena of doing something with our new understanding. The challenge for each reader lies in making the connection between what a learning combination is and what its meaning brings to the classroom. What has been accomplished in the first four chapters of this book is awareness. The reader is now aware of the interaction of our learning system (cognition, conation, and affectation), aware of the interaction of our learning patterns, and aware that these are easily observable manifestations of learning behaviors within the classroom. However, awareness is only the first level of involvement in the Let

AUTHOR'S NOTE: Individuals who contributed case studies for use in this chapter are Esther Biermann, Michael Buccialia, Sandra Dorrell, Mary Beth Foster, Tammy Gambone, and Mary Ann Hilbert.

Me Learn Process. Being open to hearing the voice of the learner is one thing; responding to it is another. This chapter presents the bridge between the reader's awareness of the learner's voice and the reader's response to the learner.

Once You Know the Let Me Learn Process, There's No Turning Back

Recently, a group of teachers with whom I have been working told me, "We wish we'd never met you! Now we can't sit down to plan a lesson without thinking first, Who are the learners in my classroom? How will what I am planning affect them? Can they take what I have planned and make this a good learning experience for them?' We were really good teachers before. Now we are really good teachers who know our learners. We have a conscience. We can't ignore what we know. This is a lot of work—but it's work that's making a difference."

The difference this group was referring to is the difference of knowing how to give the learner

- Word tools to communicate with others about learning
- An active opportunity to grow rather than a passive place to vegetate
- A place to develop life skills of communication, cooperation, and respect

Where Do You Begin to Make a Difference?

Making a difference begins the moment you identify and confirm your own learning combination. Over and over again, people who have completed the Learning Combination Inventory remark, "Now I understand why . . . *why* school was so easy; *why* school never made sense to me; *why* I didn't care about memorizing vocabulary; *why* my notebook was never organized; *why* building dioramas never appealed to me . . . why . . . why . . . why . . . because my learning combination is such that I learn best when . . ." At that point, the blinders come off, the insight is clear, and the learning voice within you finds expression.

Not long ago, a teacher with more than 15 years' experience came to me and said, "I just want you to know what being in this course has meant to me. For the first time, I haven't felt dumb. My husband and son have always overpowered me with their facts and information. I could never understand why I didn't appreciate information as they did. I thought there was something wrong with me. But beginning with the very first class session, when I completed the LCI and learned who I was as a learner, I have felt so much better about myself. So much more capable. I really achieved this semester because I knew I, too, was a real learner, and that my combination of patterns was just as important and just as useful as those of the other members of the class. I'm forty years old, and I finally know I learn well too!"

The point of relating this incident is simply to emphasize that this adult learner's sense of freedom and empowerment can be repeated over and over again within any classroom. The place where this emancipation of learning begins is with the teacher. Once the teacher knows his or her learning combination, then he or she is ready to help the learners within the classroom to have the same experience. The steps of this process are not complicated:

- Administer the LCI to each student.
- Check the comments and scale scores.
- Allow the students to learn each others' learning combinations.
- Anticipate the learning patterns that are going to be required for each learning activity.
- Include learners in the planning of learning activities (rubrics, portfolios, standards for performance assessment).
- Allow students to pair up, form groups, or work alone.
- Allow students to negotiate the assignment's requirements.
- Build time within each learning unit for reflection on how learning occurred for the students.
- Analyze the nature of the learning that occurred and the outcomes in terms of life skills, communication, cooperation, and respect.

As a result of these actions, the teacher and learners begin to create an alliance. No more fear of the unknown; no more reaction to what was previously thought of as "foreign" learning behaviors. Instead, there is an exchange of learning gifts. "This is what I bring to any learning activity. What do you bring? How can we make the differences work? How can we learn from the difference?" The teacher and students agree to talk to one another; they agree to allow some things to be different. This is a period of cautious investigation. As one teacher explained,

I'm understanding how students' frustrations can come from working on assignments I give that are outside of their "Use First" or "Use as Needed" combinations. I'm learning to be more comfortable with students demonstrating what they know by using alternative assignments. If students can give me a good solid reason why they need to change an assignment, I will accommodate them. I was never like that before. I've learned an awful lot about my students and myself, and I've changed because of it.

Change in how we see our students and how we work with them occurs over time. It begins with asking, "What will work? What doesn't work as well?" There is some trial and error; some experimentation with different ways of doing learning. Throughout this early period of the Let Me Learn Process, there is an emphasis on listening—listening to the voices of the learners as they talk to each other about learning. The teacher needs to be prepared to hear the subtle and the not-so-subtle messages of resistance, growth, and success.

> Six-year-old to his teacher: Mrs. Ryan, you do let us do lots of different things now to show what we know, but we still always have to do them your way, step-by-step.
>
> Trevor (highly confluent and avoids sequential) to Nick (highly sequential and highly technical): OK, so you showed me how to do this step-by-step, but while you were taking your time to do it that way, I had figured out how to do it ten times faster my own way.
>
> Nick (with an exasperated and bewildered look): But you need to learn how to do it this way too! Sometimes you need to follow the directions just as they are.

My Learning Combination Isn't an Illness to Be Cured

It is easy for us to fall into the trap of wanting to change others to be more like us. This is especially true for teachers. Teachers are eager to teach those students who are not highly sequential or precise how to "overcome" this shortcoming. The teacher's intention is good, if not well-founded. Our learning patterns form a unique combination that interacts to make us who we are as learners. They are not a sign of our inability. They are, instead, a sign of our true potential. As such, they should be recognized, valued, and celebrated. When we seek to help students use patterns that they would otherwise avoid, we are asking them to stretch themselves to accommodate "foreign ways" of doing their learning. This is not an unhealthy exercise, unless the motivation behind it is to change the learner into a clone of ourselves, thereby making teaching easier and the student more acceptable to us. When we seek to change people for our sake, we are behaving inappropriately.

Here, once again, we are confronted by our biases. Precise means more correct answers; avoidance of precise means the student doesn't know anything. Sequential means more attention to what I want done; avoidance of sequential means undisciplined learning. Use of technical means not in tune with the academic agenda; avoidance of technical is not a concern and, in fact, goes unnoticed in most classroom settings. Confluence means lots of arguments about following directions, whereas avoidance of confluence means cooperation and quiet compliance.

Therefore, as teachers, we think we should seek to raise a student's ability to use the first two learning patterns (sequential and precise) and seek to dissuade the student from using the latter two (technical and confluent) because they are disruptive to our educational process. Our agenda becomes one of conversion. The teacher wants to convert the learner into a *real* learner as defined by traditional classroom practices and standardized assessments. However, as teachers and educators, we are not in the business of education to change students' learning patterns. We are in the service of education to facilitate student growth on the basis of their aptitude and unique combination of learning patterns. Anything more than that is meddling; anything less than that is dereliction of duty.

Alternatives to Conversion

Clearly, there is much to be learned from observing other learners, asking questions, and paying attention to how the person does what he or she does. Given sufficient time and space, these interactions can foster a growth in understanding. They can increase the learners' appreciation for each other, resulting in respect and peace within the classroom. This appreciation can be expressed by such causal declarations as, "Hey, Eddie, you aren't so weird after all," or in sophisticated analyses of group interactions, such as that of 8-year-old Rachel, who surmised, "I think I need to work in that group next time, Ms. Baehr, because they're too different. Wesley is so precise, and Kyle avoids it. Mark argues with Wesley about directions, and Kyle leaves the group because he is so technical, he needs to get away. My scores show I'm a 'bridge' person, and that's what that group needs. I can help them to learn to understand each other."

We Are Not in the Business of Takeovers: We Are in the Business of Forming Partnerships

Facilitating learning within the child is the primary responsibility facing every classroom teacher. As the opening quote to this chapter suggests, we teachers should be developing experiences in which we can mutually engage with the learner. These mutual experiences can be structured opportunities in each child's daily routine that will enable him or her to experience feelings of competence, belonging, usefulness, efficacy, and optimism.

Partnerships Come in Many Forms

Forming partnerships isn't easy. Solid learning partnerships are not the result of random assignments or the pairing of like minds. Forming a true learning partnership requires knowing oneself as a learner, listening to who others are, weighing the differences, and considering what those differences mean in terms of working together. Partnerships require work, patience, and most of all, commitment. As the teacher models this with learners in the classroom, the modeling becomes the framework by which students learn to work and encourage one another.

Because a major purpose of the LCI is to begin a learner-teacher dialogue, the activities that follow the student's completion of the LCI are focused on establishing dialogue. The goal is to create an atmosphere in which the learner can negotiate and discuss learner-specific strategies for adapting his or her combination of patterns to the learning requirements. Thus, the LCI not only identifies the learner's interactive patterns, but it also provides a voice of empowerment for the learner. This involves the teacher and student in establishing mutual understanding and respect through partnership. Hence, the LCI not only provides a place to start that can be within the comfort zone of the learner but also facilitates the student moving into more challenging assignments with a new confidence.

The Let Me Learn Process
Is a Let Me Learn Partnership

What does all of this suggest concerning the process required for developing true learning partnerships? It suggests that having the teacher understand the learner as a learner—and having the teacher and student work together as partners—holds great potential for the long-term facilitation of student learning. Carl Glickman's (1991) point is well taken. "Teachers need to think about how students think, listen to them describe what helps them learn, and share with their colleagues activities and methods that get closer to active learning in the manner in which the students describe how they learn" (p. 6). Or as one teacher wrote, "The integrity of teaching is in doing what is best for the student regardless of the current trend, the administration's need for documentation or pressure from the community. Our paramount responsibility is to the learner. We must be open to their way of doing things, their interests and their needs. Only by empowering the learner can we teach in the truest sense of the word."

The latest educational research supports the partnership concept. We know that when students work with adults who continue to view themselves as learners, students are more likely to demonstrate successful learning behaviors. A case in point is Ms. P., a fifth-grade teacher with 13 years' experience, who declared to her fellow faculty members, "I can now see how children, especially those who are different than I am, approach learning. Now that I recognize some of their values and some of what they'd prefer to do, I can be more understanding and more flexible as a teacher. I've also allowed them to see me as a learner, and we can help each other and give each other strategies. Sometimes I tell them how I would approach a problem. Sometimes, when I write, I tell them how I'm doing it or how I organize my work. I am very sequential and precise. I have a boy who is extremely confluent and technical, who is one of my lowest scores in precise, and we work very quietly together. I show him some strategies I use. We discuss how we each do things in school because they are comfortable for us."

What Do We Do After We Have Tuned In to the Voice?

When we read episodes such as this, we recognize that having information about a student's combination of learning patterns is the place to begin understanding how a child learns. The following pages relate how teachers have successfully built partnerships with students of various ages who use various learning combinations.

The Enigma

Sean, an elementary student whose mother was beside herself, asked his teacher for help. The teacher administered the LCI to Sean, and her observations about him were confirmed. Sean's LCI scores (Sequential, 24; Precise, 25; Technical, 35; and Confluent, 26) helped explain why he has been such a puzzlement to her. "He hates all written assignments but is very verbal and likes to share many things. He'd rather build or make things. He loves to tell stories. He went to Disney World with his family and showed five pictures to the class. It took him 45 minutes. Every picture involved him discussing everything that happened before the picture and everything after the picture. And because he's very dramatic, the kids loved it.

"He has a desk that's with his group and a desk that's separate. I gave him a second desk not as a punishment but because we had discussed this. When he was with the rest of the group, he'd get nothing

done because the rest of them distracted him, according to Sean. So I gave him another desk to sit at when he chose, and he has completed a lot more while he's been there. Over time, he's gotten better at interacting with the rest of the students.

"Another strategy that Sean and I came up with was to allow him to be out of his seat if he were quiet and didn't disturb others. One day I looked up, and he was quietly walking back and forth at the rear of the room. He had completed his work and was waiting for others to complete theirs. Instead of being fidgety and distracting others, he decided to use our stretch time strategy. I approached him after a few moments and asked if everything was all right. "Oh, no problem. I'm just wondering and pondering," he said. I felt then that we had reached a new level of comfortable communication and trust.

"When I looked at Sean's LCI's scores and saw that he scored so technically, I was able to understand why I was seeing the "loner" aspect of him. I knew he could learn, but his formal written work was just awful. It was so little in amount. Because of that, I developed the strategy with him of using tapes. When we first had an essay test, I knew what he had written on the test wasn't what he knew about the material. So I talked to him about it, and he said that when he wrote, he realized he wrote too much, and he wouldn't have enough time to finish the last question, and his hand was already beginning to hurt him. He said he was going back to the first question to finish, but he ran out of time. Sean was caught between the demands of his preciseness (25) and his technicalness (35). He knew a great deal of information, but writing it was not the answer for him.

"Because I knew that highly technical learners prefer to show what they know by telling the teacher rather than using paper or pencil, I thought, here's an opportunity to see if that is true. So when he was to take a test that required lots of written answers, I would send him into an adjourning classroom with a tape recorder and the test. He was to respond on the tape, and I would later listen to the tape and grade his responses. I thought the audiocassettes would come out disjointed, but he carefully read the question on the tape, announcing its number first. Then he would speak at length. His answers were phrased exactly as if they were written, but they were much more complete than if he had to write them. And I told him, after a few times of this, he would have to take the tape home and transcribe it. In that way, he could have unlimited time to write out the answers for me. He was very happy with that arrangement. He also could use the computer to type out his transcriptions. As a result of this strategy, his social studies grade changed remarkably. I have shared this approach with another of his teachers, and she intends to use it also. She was amazed at how much Sean knew and was able to share on tape but not in a standard written-testing mode.

"Working with Sean in this manner has changed my perception of him enormously. He is a child who needs to see the big picture and needs space and a place to be off by himself to recharge and regroup. He is a very capable learner who is becoming a more successful student."

The One Who Drives Me Nuts

Alex's highly precise and sequential teacher explained Alex in this manner:

"He's a very capable student, but his writing scores are very poor, and he usually shuts down at a writing assignment. He loves to express himself through art, but even the quality of the art isn't very good. He is comfortable talking in front of a group and sharing his ideas, even when they are way out there. Sometimes, his ideas have nothing to do with what we are talking about, but he is always excited about his idea, so I thought his scores would be highly confluent. I was correct as his scores indicated (Sequential, 19; Precise, 15; Technical, 34; and Confluent, 26). However, his technical score surprised me. Once I knew his entire combination, I understood him better. His written answers to 'What frustrates me most?' was 'I don't like writing a lot.' 'I would make myself a project,' to show how he learned, and he would 'build a diorama or 3-d projects that had to do with what we learned.' After seeing the scores and reading the responses, two things were very clear to me: Alex and I have opposite learning combinations (Mine is Sequential, 24; Precise, 28; Technical, 15; and Confluent, 19); and we would have our work cut out for us if we were going to form a teacher-learner partnership!

"Every marking period, the boys and girls in my class have to give a book report to their small group. My kids work on it at home and then bring it in. They bring in props, but it is usually a minor part of the project. Alex, however, spent three whole choice-time periods (a total of 1½ hours) working on his project. It was driving me crazy, but I thought I should let him do it. I thought he was spending too much time building this creation, but it really helped him understand the story. The written work of the project was horrible, and we need to work on that. But it was clear to me early on that allowing him to do the building of the set was vital to his succeeding on his book report. For someone like him (Sequential, 19; and Precise, 15), this "setup," as he called it, would help him recount the detail he needed to tell the story in sequence. I truly believe that without this elaborate prop, he would not have done as well as he did."

She later said, "As difficult as it was, he wouldn't have been able to follow along without this thing [the 3-ft.-by-2-ft. diorama consisting of a forest with trees, a large winding pathway, and a turreted castle with two distinct sides and entrances]. I have learned that I need to be more

Transcription of Alex's Amazing Castle
Book Report–Video

This is the story of the boy who fooled the dragon. Here's the setup I made of the story. First, there were two sons who lived in this wood cabin. One day, the father had enough, and he kicked them out. When the King heard about this, he sent his guards out to get the older son who was known for doing wonderful tricks. The guards came running out of the castle, and they said, "You have to go get the white horse in the dragon's castle."

[Alex manually shifts the castle to show its other side reflecting a different door and representing the other King's castle. This is his inventive way of doing a 2-in-1 structure. He does not miss a beat in his storytelling as he shifts from one castle-front to the other. The fact that the turrets fall down each time he does this does not cause him concern. He replaces them and keeps right on talking.]

When he went to the dragon's castle the horse made a little noise and woke the dragon up. He looked down and gave the horse a whack because he woke him up. Luckily Larrick was in there, but the dragon didn't know this. So as the horse ran by where he was hiding, Larrick took the reins and rides off to the King's castle. When he got to the King's castle, he gave him the horse. And then the King said, "You have to go get the magic blanket." So he went back to the dragon's castle. But this time he got caught and the dragon seized him. He decided to keep him until morning to cook him for dinner.

Well, Larrick played another trick. When the dragon's wife was going to cook him, he pushed the wife into the boiling pot of water. Then he stole the magic blanket and came back to the King's castle. And then the King said, "You have to get me one last thing, the dragon's head." "But on one condition," Larrick said, "That you make your daughter my wife." The King thought nobody would be able to do that, but Larrick knew a few tricks. So Larrick accepted the offer and stayed in the forest for a bit. Then when the dragon came there, Larrick had this orangey beard so the dragon didn't know [him]. Larrick had a box with him. When the dragon came over to where Larrick was, Larrick said the dragon couldn't fit in the box. The dragon disagreed and climbed into the box. So Larrick put the lid on. Once the dragon was in there, it was pretty tight, but Larrick pressed hard. He wanted to put more pressure on there so the dragon wouldn't come out. He brought the box back to the King. When the King opened the box, he got pulled in, and the dragon ate him.

Then Larrick came, and he married the King's daughter, and she became his wife, and he became King.

The End.

Exhibit 5.1

patient and let him build those things, and he has learned that he needs to talk with me about how he learns." Teacher-learner partnerships begin in this way.

The One I Can't Reach . . . But Did

For Leon, assignments were a lost cause. He literally lost track of everything—time, materials, directions, and interest in learning. His report card consisted of Ds and Fs. His LCI scores (Sequential, 15; Precise, 26; Technical, 30; and Confluent, 19) indicated his avoidance of sequence and his reliance on his technical reasoning. With that information in hand, his teacher and he began to strategize. He teamed up with a highly sequential student who helped him organize himself. His teacher describes the transformation:

> *He has learned to seek advice on how to begin assignments and how to meet deadlines. He has a special place where he keeps his most important papers, and he now carefully records his assignments in his assignment book—something he simply didn't do before! He has also learned to feel successful by demonstrating his knowledge through his technical skills. On the River Run Wild Project, he chose to construct a diorama that he completed on time and that met all the requirements. This was a first! In the cooperative group project, he took pride in constructing a bridge. I could see how comfortable he felt working with the tools. He got great feedback from the group, too!*

There is no doubt that at his stage in his development as a student, he will continue to need a lot of time to complete assignments. He frustrates easily when given written assignments, but if he continues with the tape recordings and things like that, I think it will help him greatly. He loves to listen and learns well when things are relevant to him. He needs three things: a partner to help him understand directions, space to move around in, and much reassurance from the teacher. With that, he will continue to succeed. One thing I know for certain is that he loves to learn! This marking period he has earned all Cs. We both feel we have succeeded. We have formed a real learning partnership.

Once We Really Understand the Learner

One of the more interesting cases of teacher partnerships occurred when three teachers sat down and discussed a particularly difficult student described by her current teacher as "domineering, subtly defiant, and intentionally aggravating." However, after her previous year's teachers and the current teacher looked at her LCI scores, they were much more able to understand this student. Ashley is a "strong-willed" learner, that is, a learner who has three LCI scores that fall into the "I Use This First" range. Often, these students are as misunderstood as the student who avoids precision or isn't sequential. Ashley is very confluent, and that is the part of her most often seen in the classroom. Her assertiveness and free spirit overshadow the other components of her learning patterns—her need to use preciseness and her need to be sequential. Her LCI scores explained her classroom behavior.

"I remember her writing last year and feeling she was trying to derail me or herself so she wouldn't have to get it done. She would spend more time asking, "What's another word for . . . ?" She would go to the thesaurus to look it up. She was checking her spelling. Now that I understand her level of preciseness, I realize her need to have exact words to describe what it was she was trying to express."

Her former math teacher added several more pieces to the puzzle of this student's learning. He openly admitted,

I did not fully appreciate or understand her. In fact, I found myself growing increasingly intolerant of her. There was this ongoing conflict when I wanted her to do her math work. She made it an extremely laborious, time-consuming, organizational task that would take a third of the class period before she would even get started. The same thing was true on a test. I interpreted that as resistance. It was only after she had taken the LCI that I recognized she is extremely precise—much more than I'd ever suspected her to be—and extremely sequential. You see, we all saw the other part of her learning pattern that was her high confluence. She could just rattle off ideas and discuss things off the top of her head. But with math, she couldn't do it. I even began to wonder if she just wasn't good at math, but then her total learning combination would kick in and all of a sudden, she'd be fine. It was the sequential and precise preparations that were extremely time-consuming as well as aggravating. So learning about her patterns was a tremendously eye-opening experience for me. What I had failed to understand about her was she would use one part of her pattern in some subjects and another part of her pattern in math. I had only been seeing one side of her, and it was the other part that I most needed to understand as her math teacher.

Her literature teacher explained,

Well, when I met her all I saw was one student who would tell you what was right or wrong. And if a student was asked a question, she would answer it for him or her. After learning her LCI scores, Ashley now

understands her own behavior, and I do too. I now know why her pa-
pers are filled with little eraser smudges because her sentences have to
be correct. And if she's using pen, she has to use White Out liquid paper
to correct her mistakes, and she won't go on until it is dry.

Using the LCI has given me an entirely different picture of Ashley.
Not only do I understand her better; she understands herself. Now I can
work with her better and so can her classmates.

The partnership of these teachers has certainly provided a helpful
frame of reference for working with Ashley in the future.

When teachers and students form partnerships based upon the knowledge of each other's learning patterns, they are able to create an atmosphere in which they have the opportunity to formulate specific techniques or strategies for using their learning patterns effectively.

Another Type of Partnership: Heads Together, Minds at Work

Learner-to-learner partnerships are a natural outgrowth of the Let Me Learn Process. Learning to listen to the voices of peers by working in cooperative pairs, groups of four, or teams is all a part of "two-getherness." Much can be learned from these arrangements. As in the traditional cooperative learning model, personal accountability and group performance are balanced. However, as an outgrowth of the Let Me Learn Process, students are placed intentionally in groups rather than randomly assigned. The purpose of structuring cooperative learning groups in this manner is to ensure that each learner has a meaningful learning experience that matches his or her learning combination. In this type of consciously configured learning community, it is the contribution that each learner makes to the team effort rather than the completion of an artificially assigned role to play (recorder, reader, etc.) that is the focus. The learner knows his or her combination, shares it with the group members, and actually participates in identifying what he or she can do for the good of the group.

Because all members of the cooperative learning group understand the difference among the members, including their scores and ranges within those scores, the group is prepared to match the work to be done to the team members' combinations. In working in this manner, the learners not only contribute to the successful outcome of the group effort but also personally affirm each member's unique contribution to the learning outcome. Students learn to ask themselves, "What am I prepared to contribute? How is my contribution valued? Am I dominating or contributing? Am I listening or controlling?"

Phase I: The Beginning

Student 3: We have three people in our group. One is highly precise and highly sequential (Student 1), one is highly sequential (Student 2), and then there's me. I'm highly confluent and pretty technical. I'm not very precise. Our project is to build a doghouse. We are supposed to draw diagrams, and we have to write an introduction.

Teacher: You've got to have a doghouse, layout, and a description. You will need to talk with one another to discuss what you want it to look like when it's all done.

Phase II: The Work

Student 2: The doghouse was just a square with a triangle roof. I drew it out, and then I cut out the pattern. We all designed it. She's writing (Student 1), and he's assembling it (Student 3).

Teacher: So how have you done in terms of your rubric?

Student 2: We are checking those now. Let's see, we need a very good diagram. Follow directions. Use appropriate material, self-control, participation equal, good construction, and realistic detail. So far, we have written material and we have good diagrams. We have done good self-control. We do have the construction, but the details are a little short.

Student 3: Do you want to have shingles?

Student 2: No, let's not do anybody else's idea.

Student 1: We have the house, a doggie door. I'll write the important things that we have. We haven't taken anybody else's ideas, we have our own ideas, stuff like that. (Dan keeps assembling the rest of the house and roof.)

Student 1: Dan, I hate to tell you this . . . but that roof doesn't look even. Yeah, that's it. Measure, measure, measure.

Exhibit 5.2

The example that is depicted in Exhibit 5.2 is based upon the experience of a sixth-grade class. The transcription of one group's "talking and listening" illustrates how cooperative learning and the Let Me Learn Process complement each other.

Putting people together can form two-getherness when they know and respect what each can contribute to the outcome. As the sixth-grade teacher explained, "I think the students learned a lot about trying to work

Code for Responsible Learning

As a result of knowing my Learning Combination, I will:

1. Value and respect the Learning Combinations of others whose learning processes are different from my own

2. Talk to my teacher and my classmates about the processes of learning that are unique to me

3. Listen to other students when they describe how they learn best

4. Discuss with my teacher or a classmate the frustrations with learning that I am experiencing rather than displaying my feelings inappropriately

5. Exercise greater patience with my teacher, my classmates, and myself as together we learn how to learn successfully

6. Help my classmates by encouraging them when they are discouraged or confused about a learning assignment

7. Work together in groups in a way that allows each member of my group to use his or her Learning Combination best

8. Put forth my best effort to demonstrate what I know in a manner that allows the maximum use of my Learning Combination

9. Grow in my willingness and ability to use those patterns of my Learning Combination that I currently avoid

10. Make a promise to myself that—each day—all year—I will be the best learner I can be!

Exhibit 5.3

together and honor each other's ideas. I was amazed at what they came up with. Watching these kids become cooperative was a real joy. When I do this again, I will insist that they take time to allow the confluent folks to generate at least three ideas that the group could use. And I would require them to allow the sequential folks to help them review the directions and make a plan before the technical learners run off to get their materials. This also would allow the precise learners to get their ideas for writing the outcome. Now I know that each of the learners can use all of the patterns but, when we start out learning to do cooperative learning, I think I would rather have the students specialize in their 'I Use This First' pattern so that everyone can have an equal responsibility."

Building a learning team in this manner allows students the opportunity to learn in a group, learn from the group, and gain confidence in what

Code for Responsible Teaching

As a result of knowing my students' Learning Combinations and my own, I will:

1. Value and respect the Learning Combinations of others whose learning processes are different from my own

2. Talk about the processes of learning using simple terms and clear examples to which students of varying ages and Learning Combinations can relate

3. Listen to the spoken and unspoken messages that students are conveying about how they learn best

4. Observe student behavior, noting the difference between behavior that is an outgrowth of frustration with learning and behavior that is intentionally disruptive

5. Exercise greater patience and more understanding of student learning behaviors that I previously found difficult to tolerate

6. Maintain high standards of performance while allowing students to use different learning processes to arrive at the same learning goal

7. Group students in order to maximize the use of their Learning Combinations

8. Assess student work by allowing students to demonstrate what they know in a manner that allows the maximum use of their Learning Combinations

9. Provide students with learning experiences that are relevant, challenging, and engaging of their learning processes

10. Make a difference—each day—all year—one learner at a time

Exhibit 5.4

they are learning and doing. They will also be prepared, when called upon later, to perform the task as an empowered, independent learner.

The Potential of Learning Partnerships

Educators need to study the potentially salient effects that forming partnerships with learners can have upon the learners' ability to initiate and sustain successful learning. Stephanie Pace Marshall (1996) eloquently describes such partnerships as "a personalized learning covenant . . . evolutionary in nature to the human learning experience and created through a mutual investment in learning."

The Let Me Learn Process is an effective vehicle for developing personalized learning covenants. In fact, the nature of these covenants has been captured by students, teachers, and Let Me Learn Process facilitators in two codes, the Code for Responsible Teaching and the Code for Responsible Learning. Those who have used the Let Me Learn Process refer to these as the building blocks of a healthy teacher-learner partnership, one that listens to and values the voice of the learner and the voice of the teacher.

And This Is What They Said

Our learning patterns form a unique combination that interact to make us who we are as learners. They are not a sign of our inability. Instead, they are a sign of our true potential. As such, they should be recognized, valued, and celebrated.

References and Selected Bibliography

Brooks, J., & Brooks, M. (1993). *The case for constructivist classrooms.* Alexandria, VA: Association for Supervision and Curriculum Development.

Caine, R., & Caine, G. (1997). *Education on the edge of possibility.* Arlington, VA: Association for Supervision and Curriculum Development.

DeAngelis, T. (1995). A nation of hermits: The loss of community. *APA Monitor, 26*(9), p. 1.

Glickman, C. (1991). Pretending not to know what we know. *Educational Leadership, 48*(4), 4-10.

James, W. (1910). *Talks with teachers on psychology: And to students on some of life's ideals.* New York: Norton.

Johnston, C. (1996). *Unlocking the will to learn.* Thousand Oaks, CA: Corwin.

Johnston, C., & Dainton, G. (1996). *The learning combination inventory.* Pittsgrove, NJ: Let Me Learn.

Marshall, S. (1996). *Dancing to the rhythm of learning.* Address to the Plenary Session of the Association for Supervision and Curriculum Development National Conference meeting, New Orleans, LA.

Palmer, P. (1983). *To know as we are known: A spirituality of education.* San Francisco: HarperCollins.

Sagor, R. (1996). Building resiliency in students. *Educational Leadership, 54*(1), 38-43.

Smith, F. (1995). Let's declare education a disaster and get on with our lives. *Phi Delta Kappan, 76,* 584-590.

Sparks, D., & Hirsh, S. (1997). Staff development, innovation and instructional development. In *A new vision for staff development*. Alexandria, VA: Association for Supervision and Curriculum Development.

Winne, P., & Marx, R. (1980). Matching students' cognitive responses to teaching skills. *Journal of Educational Psychology, 72*, 257-264.

Further Reading

Costa, A. (1981). Teaching for intelligent behavior. *Educational Leadership, 39*(1), 29-31.

Hesselbein, F., et al. (1997). *Creating sustainable communities for the twenty-first century.* San Francisco: Jossey-Bass.

Part II

Tuning In to the Voices of Those Who Have Listened and Learned

Does Let Me Learn really work? And if so, how can I make it work for me in my classroom? My school? In the following chapters, teachers and administrative leaders present the approaches they used as they learned to listen to the voices of students, parents, and colleagues.

The integrity of teaching is in doing what is best for the student regardless of the current trend, the administration's need for documentation or pressure from the community. Our paramount responsibility is to the learner. We must be open to their way of doing things, their interests and their needs. Only by empowering the learner can we teach in the truest sense of the word.

Kathy Whitmore
Personal reflection, June 22, 1997
Rowan University

6

Listening to the Elementary Learner: Plans for Success

My professional experience is based in the elementary world, a world in which the use of words, wonder, and stories is central. It is in this environment that teaching and learning ideas are told, repeated, and modified in the finest of "oral traditions." There is no teacher-learner environment in which more interpersonal, intergenerational sharing occurs than in an elementary school building.

I have chosen "oral tradition" to tell my Let Me Learn experience because I have seen how the ideas of a single teacher can grow and develop into a very powerful set of learning experiences. The process is a simple but amazing one. A teacher involved in the Let Me Learn Process generates an idea. The teacher experiments with it and then shares it with another teacher. They talk, they discuss, they reflect. Then the idea becomes a part of the second teacher's idea bank. He or she then builds on, enhances, modifies, and implements the idea. Having achieved the "seal of approval" for making a difference with learners, the teaching/learning idea takes on a life of its own as it is shared with still more teachers.

The best part of the Let Me Learn oral tradition, in my experience, is that no teacher has taken an idea and left it in the same form as it was received. Each has put his or her own spin on it, shaped it, and honed it to suit the age and the understanding of the learner.

AUTHOR'S NOTE: This chapter is the voice of Pat Maher. It presents the view of an elementary teaching consultant who tells the story of elementary teachers as they implemented the Let Me Learn Process within their classrooms. Individuals and groups who contributed case studies for use in this chapter are Anne Baehr, Gwen Barnes, Barbara Barycki, Karen Bennett, Esther Biermann, Rich Cali, Deena Chando, JoAnn Corvino, Heidi Daunoras, Paul Flesher, Jo Anne Glass, Lynne Glickman, Laura Hammond, Ann Hostetter, Ann Hull, Lynn Kline, Joyce LaPlante, Susan Little, Helen McCracken, Karen Mikle, Peggy Novicki, Susan Ryan, Evelyn Sabo, Nancy Sheppard, Susan Stone, Paulette Taylor, Luella Vengenock, Monica Wells, Linda Wittmann, and the 1997 sixth-grade class of Alloway Public School.

Why Not a Cookbook?

Because most elementary school teachers are highly sequential and highly precise, it would be easy for this chapter to become a recipe book feeding the most predominant learning combination of teachers. However, that would defeat the empowering effect of the Let Me Learn Process. During a conversation with several elementary teachers and administrators, the issue of a "cookbook" chapter versus a general overview of activities arose. What ensued was a discussion about class-specific versus template teaching. It was the consensus of those who had used the Let Me Learn Process that one of its positive aspects was the manner in which the process encouraged teachers to use their professional decision making to develop their own lessons.

Each member of the discussion was very clear that he or she would rather take a concept, idea, or previously successful teaching lesson and model and shape it into his or her own. After all, ownership in teaching is as important as ownership in learning. Just as we want learners to discover their learning combination, we need to respect the teacher's right and potential for developing his or her own teaching combination.

Therefore, what follows are the stories of teachers, not their lesson plans. Along the way, the reader will see examples of student work product and will hear the voices of teachers talking about what worked well for them. What the reader will soon surmise is that teachers, when given the opportunity to know themselves as well as their students as learners, can and will act to do all within their power to provide a healthy and nurturing learning environment. These are the stories of those who have done just that.

Introducing Let Me Learn Into the Primary Classroom

There is no question that preparing elementary learners to complete the LCI is more involved than preparing older students. The younger the children, the more preparation and discussion is needed before taking the LCI. The most successful administrations of the LCI occurred when the teachers provided ample opportunities for the students to explore how and where we use our brains to learn. The goal is to break the mold that restricts students to thinking that learning occurs only in school and that learning is done in only one way.

Linda's Story

Linda is a first-grade teacher whose story is a story of success in launching the Let Me Learn Process with very young children.

Exhibit 6.1

I remember my first insight into a child's learning combination. It was early in my involvement with Let Me Learn. I gave my students a math paper that had a drawing box at the top. I told them to ignore it. To help them remember to skip the top, I had the children place a giant "X" across that part of the page. No sooner had I said to do this than Amy raised her hand and said, "We don't have to do the top, right?" and I said, "No, Amy." And she said, "OK."

Five minutes later she raised her hand and said, "Are you sure we don't have to do the top?" And I said, "No, sweetie, really." Two minutes later, she raised her hand again and asked, "Can I do the top?" I turned to my teaching aide and said, "Now let's guess what Amy's learning combination is?" We both laughed.

Prior to being a part of the Let Me Learn Process, I would not have understood Amy's sequentialness or her need to do her work from beginning to end even if the work wasn't assigned! Now I knew. I understood, and I could silently enjoy the persistence of her need to use her learning combination.

Linda Begins the Let Me Learn Process

I actually didn't think that 6-year-olds would understand the Learning Combination concept. I thought it would be much more difficult to talk

Exhibit 6.2

to children about their brain and learning, but the first day we talked about learning, the children came up with, "Well, I learn if I go to a museum," or, "Oh, I learn from reading," "I learn from my Mom," "I learned to ride my bike." I just mentioned the word *learn*, and they just went on and on with it. I was very surprised. I thought the majority of the children would say they learn while they are sitting in my class, or they learn while they are doing their work, but they didn't at all. What I discovered is that children have a great understanding of where learning takes place. They see learning as going far beyond the school site, the classroom, or their desks! I honestly thought that they would say things purposely to please me, and they didn't at all. They taught me how interested they are in how they learn and how much they understand about themselves as learners.

The Fascinating Brain

After the introductory lessons on where we learn, I taught the children about the interaction of our brain. I used the terms, "I think," "I do," and "I feel" in place of the more sophisticated terms *cognition, conation,* and *affectation.* I had one little girl who was trying to describe the interaction of these to everyone else. She kept explaining, "You know like I think, I do, I feel, and it's all connected, and this is how we feel and it doesn't matter

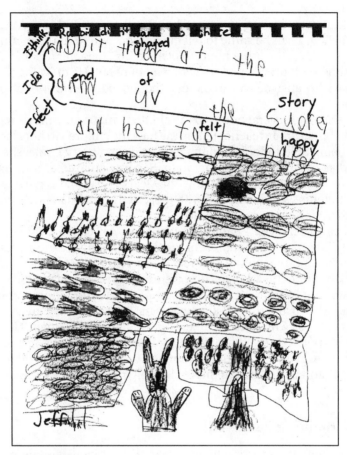

Exhibit 6.3

if everyone is different, and that's OK. Remember like Pooh is different than Tigger."

We had just read the story "Winnie the Pooh, Someone Won't Share," and all of the children had different feelings about the fact that Rabbit would not share. To reinforce these interactions and to personalize them to the students, I had them fold a sheet of manila paper into three parts and label each one with "I think," "I do," or "I feel." The children were instructed to pretend that they were a character in the story and tell what the character thought, what the character did, and then how the character felt. It was interesting to see how the children responded. Some used the pictures provided and colored the character, staying right in the lines. Some explained in paragraph form, and others drew pictures first and wrote one-word answers.

Evan drew his response to what the character was thinking, doing, and feeling. Then he came to tell me one-on-one what the picture represented. Jeff, on the other hand, explained his character first in paragraph form and then drew a picture with a lot of detail. He drew the picture on the back because he wrote so much that he didn't have enough space on the front.

I also read several books to the children about the brain. I remember another first-grade teacher telling me how the children in her class fought over being able to look through and read the library books she had selected as references about the brain. She was amazed at how interested they were in learning about how they learn. I had the same experience. The students were fascinated with these activities! I had really underestimated their interest in this topic!

A simple activity I had the students do was called a "noodle brain," and it allowed them to represent the brain's interactive processes (I think = cognition; I do = conation; I feel = affectation) using macaroni. I later noted that students whose scores were high in precision tended to pile the macaroni in heaps as if more macaroni represented more information. Those who used their sequence "First" formed very neat patterns, whereas those who used technical reasoning "First" actually "built" connections between the macaroni pieces, "chaining" them together.

As a result of completing these activities, I had a solid understanding of the childrens' interest in this topic. I felt the children were ready for the next step.

Preparing to Take the LCI

I began preparing the students to take the LCI by having them practice making decisions using the same continuum of words that appears on the LCI. We began by making five circles with the words, "Never Ever, Almost Never, Sometimes, Almost Always, and Always" within each circle. I laminated the continuum strip and taped it to each student's desk. Then the fun began!

We talked about all types of things we make decisions about. We first used food as our topic. Our first exercise in using the continuum was choosing which toppings we would want on our pizza; then what green vegetables we would or would not eat; and finally what ice cream flavors we would choose first. I would read a particular food listed on the board and ask the students to put an "X" in the circle that represented if they would "Never Ever," "Almost Never," "Sometimes," "Almost Always," or "Always" choose this. After practicing with these, we brainstormed all types of sports and wrote them on the board. Most of the boys wrote that they would never ever dance or do ballet! I thought it was interesting that a lot of them put swimming under "sometimes" because "sometimes they swim in the summer and sometimes they don't."

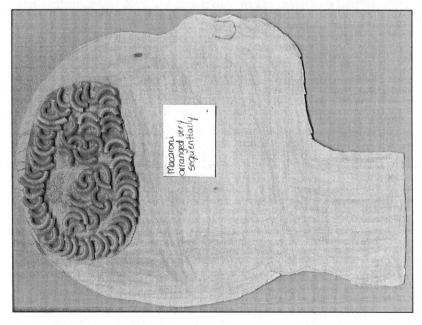

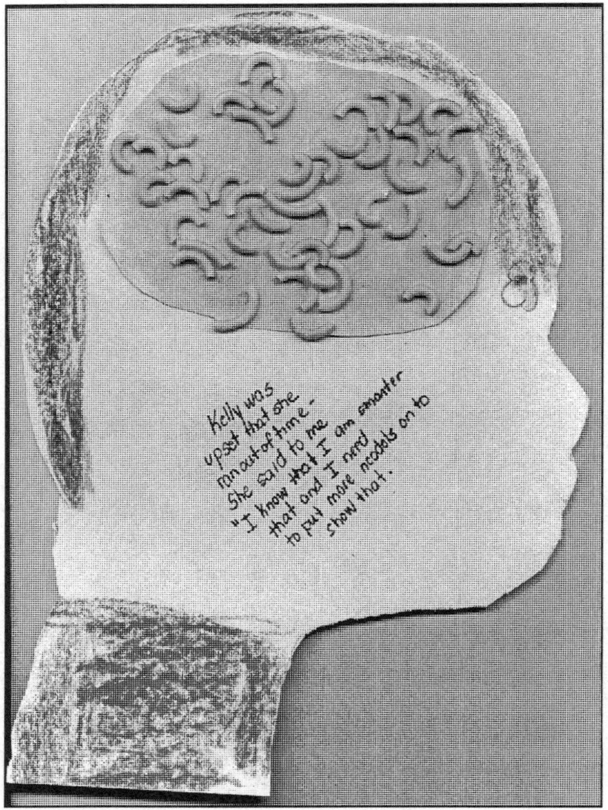

Exhibit 6.5

Exhibit 6.4

By having their own continuum in front of them, they really had to think through the difference among the five choices. I could see they were really thinking because it took them a very long time. One little boy, whose LCI scores later bore out the fact that he is highly precise, took so long to make his decisions that he didn't get to draw the pictures in the circles. He had to know exactly what he was doing. For example, he wasn't sure about the "Almost Never" category. Finally he wrote the word *running* because as he said to me, "I have asthma. I don't run. I almost never run, but sometimes I have to in gym, but that would be sometimes." I could really "hear" the kind of process he was going through to discern the difference among the choices.

Helping Children Understand That This Is a Measure, Not a Test

In anticipation of actually administering the LCI, I talked to the children about its content and appearance. I explained that I was going to ask them questions, and that their answers would give me a better idea of how they learn. I had taken an egg carton and labeled five cups with the choices, "Always," "Almost Always," "Sometimes," "Almost Never," and "Never Ever." I gave the children a chip and had them physically put the chip in the cup that had the answer they chose on it. I wanted the children to be relaxed and see this as a "fun" experience, so before beginning, I had them practice with several fun decisions. I would read a sentence, such as "I like to eat chocolate ice cream," and then have them put a chip in the egg carton cup that matched their choice of answer. I followed that with "I use bubbles in my bath"; "orange is my favorite color"; "I eat cherries on my sundaes"; and "I play baseball."

When I determined that they were confident in their decision making, I began to formally administer the LCI. To do this, I took each child individually and read the LCI statements and open-ended questions to each. Although doing it in this manner took time, it yielded very accurate responses to the questions. The students really seemed to enjoy the process.

Integrating the LCI Results

I was pleasantly surprised at how easy it was for me to verify the accuracy of the students' scores. I needed only to recall incidents that occurred during our lessons on learning or look at the students' work product to find validation of their scores. For example, as I was explaining the difference among the four learning patterns, Dominic raised his hand and asked if there was a book he could look at that had this information in it. One look at his LCI scores and I knew why he had to be in charge of his own information about this topic. His score in precision told it all! Laura, who is highly precise, was making her "noodle brain." She asked for more noodles because I hadn't given her enough. Then she asked for yellow paper because she needed to make a ponytail because that was how her hair was done that day. She drew an ear, eyelashes, and an eyebrow and then colored her brain gray because we had referred earlier to the brain as our gray matter. Her "noodle head" was filled with details—a clear reflection of her use of precision "First."

Amy, who asks for specific directions all day long, listened carefully to every question on the LCI and truly debated which answer to pick. Every question that dealt with needing or following directions, she immediately picked "Always." Every question that dealt with doing it her own way, she quickly answered "Never Ever" or "Almost Never" and added, "I would much rather have directions." The final confirmation of her scores came when I looked back at the picture she had drawn of where she learns. There before me was our classroom, just as it appeared the day we completed the assignment. She duplicated everything, even what was on the board that day!

My favorite example of "instant verification," however, occurred when I was administering the LCI to Nathan, the student I had chosen to study under the title of "the one who drives me nuts." From the very first, he answered every item about building things with an "Always." Then he invented a way to flick the answer chip into the proper cup he wanted! It wasn't difficult to see that he uses his technical reasoning "First."

Talking to Children
About Other LCI Results

After the LCI was completed, I had a private meeting with each child to discuss his or her learning combination. In class, we talked about our scores. I made a point to use the names of the four interactive patterns and stress that every combination of patterns is exciting. As follow-up activities, the students made a lock that listed their own "combination" and decorated the lock the way they wished. The children also made their own "keys" with their learning combination on them and placemats about their understanding of themselves as learners.

Since learning about our learning patterns, we find occasions each day to relate them to our classroom activities. For example, one day, a student brought in a book, *Billy and the Bad Teacher,* and asked me to read it to the class. The story is of a little boy who thought that his teacher was bad because he was late all the time and very disorganized. The little boy decided to make a list each time the teacher failed to be neat, organized, or on time. As Billy's list grew longer, he began to recognize that there were many things his teacher did that were very different and very special. Billy concluded that his teacher wasn't right or wrong, just different. In class, we discussed the contrast between Billy's and his teacher's learning processes.

Since then, there have been many times when I have paused and thought about my new insights into the students' learning. I find myself able to explain the children's learning processes to their parents in a more understandable manner.

I truly believe and have reported to the parents that these children have a much better understanding of themselves and others. They are tolerant of each other and their differences. They are much more understanding of those who need more directions or those who ask questions all day long. I feel I am more aware of why they act the way they do. The Let Me Learn Process has really helped the children see that they could be different than I am, and it would be okay.

Introducing Let Me Learn in the Upper Elementary Classroom

Lynne's Story, Grade 5

I was nervous about beginning this process with my students. I wasn't certain I knew enough about how the brain works to be able to answer their questions. I now recognize that my level of precision caused me to be concerned about having the right answers for the questions my students would ask. As it turned out, they never asked the detailed questions I feared they might! As a resource, I turned to a science teacher for help. She actually introduced the topic of the brain and how it functions. Then I picked up on the various ways we learn, finishing with the "I think, I do, I feel" interaction.

During our third class session on learning, I talked about the importance of using our brain to help us make decisions, make choices, and identify the differences among things. We then began practicing our decision making. Because my students are 11 and 12 years old, I felt they needed to practice using topics that are relevant to their lives. For example, I made up 20 statements such as, "I like to go to school," "I like to play with animals," "I like to write," "I like to ride my bike," "I like to follow directions," "I like to talk on the phone," "I like to play board games," "I like to read scary stories," "I like to please my parents," "I like to be by myself," and "I like to take care of people."

When we went over the students' choices, I said, "Well, one person had an "Always" for this and another had a "Never Ever," and that's OK." Then we talked about why it was all right to have different answers to these questions. It was a great way to see how we are each different, and that different answers to these questions didn't make one student "right" and another "wrong."

Once we completed talking through the importance of differences in choices, I had the students complete the LCI. I knew they were ready to think and choose their answers as individuals.

They Said, She Said

After administering, scoring, and verifying the results, we talked about what they could do if they had difficulty understanding an assignment or the subject we were studying. Because I am highly precise, I immediately suggested the students ask more questions. This was not their solution! The reason for this rebuff of my approach soon became very clear. The students' mean score in the use of precision was significantly below mine.

I chose to use a math lesson as a means of having the students understand their composite learning combination. In doing this, we were able to "get a handle" on possible conflicts between my approach to instruction and the students' response to it. The topic was graphing. I decided to use the students' actual scale scores to form a "human" graph. First, we established the range of scores within the class for each of the four patterns. For example, to establish the range of scores in the use of sequence, I had the students line up from lowest scale score in sequence to highest. When more than one student had the same score, students stood side by side. In doing so, they could see the modal score forming. By using the scores of a real and personal set of data, the class on graphing came alive with interest.

Next, the students took a sheet with each class member's scale scores for sequence written on it, and using their calculators, they computed the mean of the score of sequence for the class. Then we talked about both the mathematical computations of how they arrived at the range, mean, median, and mode. Finally, and most importantly, we discussed what these numbers meant for the class. It was then that we had the answer to why the class as a whole would not seek to use questioning as a means of helping them learn. After all, they had just established the class range, median, and mode for precise processing, and it was clear that this class would do better if they were allowed to use more sequential approaches (no student avoided the pattern of sequence, whereas several avoided the pattern of precision). These students, as a group, needed more examples. They asked to have whatever they were learning explained in more than one way. They needed time to think and time to complete their work. Being put on the spot for a specific answer when they still did not feel comfortable with the math process they were learning caused them to feel unsuccessful and frustrated. Through all of this, I have learned that once you have students' LCI scores, you can begin to understand what is going on inside them.

Some Reflections of the Story Gatherer

As I collected teacher stories, I recognized that students' first impressions of their learning pattern is a critical point in the process. A fourth-grade teacher observed, "Some of the children thought certain patterns were better than others. Children with a high use of sequence seemed to get the positive attention and good grades. The students who used technical and confluence 'first' seemed to feel that they were less likely to succeed in learning because they do things differently." My response to her was, "You can help reverse this negative interpretation by how you respond to the children. These children didn't develop this perspective outside of school. They learned this in school."

You can begin to reverse this misinterpretation by how you explain students' learning combinations to them. This is a great place to share your learning combination! Be sure to let them know how you answered the questions and how your responses relate to your overall learning profile. When I share what my learning combination is, I say to students:

My learning combination is Sequential, 19; Precise, 15; Technical, 24; and Confluent, 31. The pattern I "Use First" is confluence. I'm happiest when I am doing many things at the same time. I enjoy working in groups and often come up with unusual or unique ways of solving problems. When I have a problem, my first choice is to talk to a lot of other people who may have had a similar situation. My second highest pattern is technical reasoning, which I use when working in my garden and which I enjoy doing myself. I use sequence as needed, but I am not naturally very organized. I do it because I know I have to, so that important things don't get lost. I avoid precision. I don't enjoy researching information. However, I do like to read fiction for enjoyment.

What makes assignments frustrating for me is too much information or the need for a lot of research. This matches my score of precision. The way I like to show what I know is to teach or perform a speech. If I were the teacher, I would make learning fun with lots of stories and real-life examples.

You can further reverse the concern that students raise about the value of their learning combinations by respecting their learning needs. For example, I have found that once students are encouraged to know about their learning combinations, they do begin to use their new awareness with great skill.

Teachers have had many eye-opening and humorous encounters with students concerning their learning combinations. An art teacher, herself highly confluent but using her precision "As Needed," began class one day by giving a typical set of directions: "Take some yarn and put it in the dye . . ." but before she could go any further, a student raised her hand and interrupted with, "Mrs. Frances, my learning combination shows that I am very precise and sequential, so please, I need to know how much yarn and how much dye, and I need to have step-by-step directions on what I am supposed to do with it." With that, another student chimed in, and before long, the teacher realized that she needed to rethink the exactness with which she ordinarily gave directions!

In other instances, the teacher has needed to talk to students about how their learning combinations were affecting their work products. A middle school teacher told me,

> *In my 5th- and 6th-grade class, my students were grouped and asked to complete a map of an area they had just studied. As each group presented its maps, I noticed that none of the groups completed the project accurately. I looked at the group's learning combinations and noticed that none of the students used precision "First." I decided to repeat the project, but prior to assigning the task again, I brought their lack of precision to their attention.*
>
> *They discussed ways that the groups could improve the accuracy of their work. This time, the projects were highly accurate. I then shared my observation with the students' math teacher, who had been frustrated with their lack of accuracy quite often.*

The Let Me Learn Process *After* the LCI

Teachers continue to be amazed at how their students resonate with learning about themselves as learners. One teacher observed, "I was afraid that this [the Let Me Learn Process] would just be another way of labeling students, but that isn't the case at all. It empowers them." A clear example of that is the middle-school classroom in which sixth-grade students made up their own list of the top 10 reasons for knowing their learning combination. Following the format of a popular late-night television program, these students wrote:

Top Ten Reasons for Knowing Your Learning Combination:

10. To have a better understanding of how you learn.
9. So the teacher can teach you better.
8. It may help you choose an occupation.
7. To help you choose courses and subjects in high school.
6. To know what kind of learning project works best for you.

5. To know what students you work best with, and why.

4. To know who to "partner up" with when you have a project to do.

3. To know what learning processes you need to strengthen in yourself.

2. To help you learn better throughout your life.

(Drumroll, please!)

1. So you'll never get "locked out" of your *learning locker!*

Cooperative Learning

Besides providing students with insights into their learning processes, Let Me Learn has helped students work together more effectively. One seventh-grade teacher felt that the LCI was extremely beneficial in grouping her students. She related the following to me:

Using the results of the inventory, I grouped my classes by learning combinations. I worked with the resource room teacher and included special needs students in the groups. After the groups were in place, I assigned activities related to our mythology. The groups began their tasks, and for the first time in 21 years, I did not hear, "I don't want so-and-so in my group."

The students realized that each person in the group possessed a unique talent or strength that they could utilize to complete the required tasks. Before we discussed how we learn and the learning combinations of our class, students were adamant that groups must be made up of the same type of learners or they would not work. Now, when asked, these same students reply, "I wish we could have done this [cooperative grouping] all along. It makes learning fun."

During an interview with students upon the completion of the project, the teacher recorded the following remarks: "The teacher used to be the biggest thing in learning. Now I depend on my teacher, other students, and me!" "It's neat that I know how other students work and it's great to have my classmates know about my way of learning. It makes working together easier."

Mini-Tales of Elementary Teachers

Sometimes, when I talk with teachers before they are involved in the Let Me Learn Process, they express a concern that the process will add to their responsibilities and the load they already bear. However, those who have used the process soon realize that this is not a new area of study. Instead, it is easily infused into all learning activities and can aid the student in learning across the curriculum. A third-grade teacher who spoke with me explained,

> *At first, I was skeptical about the approach [Let Me Learn]. I was concerned about adding another area to an already overcrowded curriculum. However, after administering the inventory and discussing the results with my children, I found that learning combinations need to be accommodated and valued within an existing curriculum. It actually enhances the curriculum.*

Teachers' Stories About Themselves

As one teacher told me,

> *I am a very sequential learner and pretty precise as well. I avoid confluence. At times, that causes battles between me and my learners, who use confluence and technical reasoning "First." But we have learned to make decisions together and found new ways to learn where everyone has an opportunity to learn according to his or her own pattern and comfort. Using the LCI has changed the way I work with my children. First, I provide alternative activities for students—I did not do that before. Second, I do not "go nuts" when confronted with children who are very, very technical and confluent.*

One of my favorite teacher mini-tales was told to me by a veteran teacher of 20 years:

> *Early on in teaching, I would try to reach all of my students in the same way. Over the years, I realized that this approach wasn't working. The LCI gave me an insight into who these children really are as learners. As a result, I have begun providing many choices for my students. Now, my grading is not a numbers game. I look at portfolios and individual efforts. I think the LCI is a real eye-opener for education.*

Teachers and Change

I also hear from elementary teachers that, as a result of the Let Me Learn Process, the students have learned to understand themselves better. That statement is followed with, "But if you want to know who has changed the most, it's me." That statement of awareness then leads to the teacher sharing insights such as,

> *I have learned why I run my class the way I do—very sequentially. I haven't always been patient with certain children. I have learned that*

I need to be less rigid and come out of my own comfort zone to meet the needs of the various learning patterns in my class. I've been expecting them to come out of their comfort zones and be more sequential. It should be a two-way process.

Learners Telling Tales About School

The Let Me Learn Process does just what it says: It lets the student learn. In the Let Me Learn Process, we are giving the children a voice through which they can communicate the kinds of activities and expectations that stimulate their desire to go the extra mile or make that extra effort. They are allowed to say, "It's hard to wait for directions" or "I'm not good at tests." As their individual combinations unfold, students sense that regardless of the results, each pattern has benefits, value, and something important to offer. They are excited and even proud of their special patterns. Even more affirming is the revelation that just because there may be a pattern that they avoid, it does not make them any less capable as a learner or less valued as a person.

Individual Student Stories

Each time I review a set of completed LCIs, I am overwhelmed at how openly children can tell us what they need to be successful learners. The excerpts of the student letters that follow tell their own stories about the learner and the Let Me Learn Process:

Dear Mr. C.,

The 6th grade took the Learning Combination Inventory to see what everyone's learning combination was. My most commonly used part of my combination is sequential. I am very organized. I do everything step-by-step. I think this project is helping me learn more and more every day. I think everyone is learning more also, sequential or not. In the future I think this will help me do better in high school and college. My process is my personal learning process.

Your friend,

Dear Mr. C.,

My Learning Combination Inventory scores are Sequential 19, Precise 22, Technical 28 and Confluent 21. We did a fun Mayan project in social studies. We made headdresses, we sacrificed, and made posters and stuff. My idea of a project is to go out and live the project. When we did the Mayan project, I wanted to go out in the woods and live it. I knew I would be a technical learner from the beginning of page one of the LCI. In the future knowing that I begin learning by using my technical pattern will help me in doing things my way.

Your friend,

A Story That Tells the Whole Story

The Let Me Learn Process is only the beginning. It is quite exciting to see how teachers have integrated this knowledge into their classroom settings. They are not only helping students define their natural learning patterns, but they are also helping their students use their abilities successfully.

Teachers have become less annoyed with the students who begin working before all directions have been completed; who ask the teachers to repeat directions just given; who ask the teacher to explain instructions in minute detail; who want to check their work frequently for correctness; or who want to be left alone while working. As one fourth-grade teacher explained, "I don't get annoyed with the students who keep asking me for more information about assignments that were well explained. I realize that they are very precise and need information to feel comfortable. It is not that they were not paying attention." A third-grade teacher agreed, saying, "I was always hesitant in allowing students the opportunity to attempt assignments without directions and examples. However, I have now learned that confluent students are risk takers and have a need to begin assignments independently."

My story of the elementary experience is filled with stories of change and growth. Because I chose to develop this chapter by using the oral tradition, I will conclude with the same—in this case, the voice of an elementary learner and a secondary teacher.

A secondary school teacher who was participating in the Let Me Learn staff development process was sitting at her kitchen table poring over her students' LCI scores. She was intent on developing "balanced" cooperative learning groups. Her son came into the room and asked what she was doing. She was so absorbed in her work that she didn't hear his question. He moved closer to see what she was doing and peered over her shoulder. The next thing she knew, he began telling her, "No, you don't want to place him there. Look, you're going to have too much technical reasoning going on and not enough sequencing."

The mother stepped aside as her son began to shift names on the paper until he was satisfied that the groups would "work." The mother was truly impressed. She had just been taught how to structure balanced groups by her 8-year-old son, whose teacher had introduced his class to the Let Me Learn Process 3 months earlier. She reported, "The groups worked great! Much better than my first attempt to put students into cooperative learning groups."

A third-grade student, empowered by the Let Me Learn Process, had used oral tradition to make a difference with learners. Now that's a story worth repeating!

And This Is What They Said

What I discovered is that children have a great understanding of where learning takes place. They see learning as going far beyond the school site, the classroom, or their desks! I honestly thought that they would say things purposely to please me, and they didn't at all. They taught me how interested they are in how they learn and how much they understand about themselves as learners.

Without being a monopolizer of information, a teacher must be a facilitator; without being a tyrant, a teacher must be firm; without being a friend, a teacher must be approachable. A teacher needs to establish a classroom that is a safe, fair, conducive place for learning.

John Evans (in Johnston, 1996, p. 95)

7

Listening to the Voice of the Learner in the Secondary Classroom: The Challenge

I begin this chapter with the following confession: I am a secondary school teacher who believes in putting the learner first. I say this from the outset because secondary school teachers who read this chapter will immediately understand the division that this declaration creates in me. I find myself daily in a warring camp: I am bombarded by state competencies, curriculum units, and learning on demand. I can never escape the specter of the state's high school exit exam or its report card that announces how my school district compares statewide on inane things such as students' quantitative scores on the SATs!

I have decided to tell my experiences in implementing Let Me Learn because what I have learned through this process is important and should be heard by other secondary teachers. I expand upon my own experience by relating the experiences of several of my secondary colleagues who have used the Let Me Learn Process to serve the learner. But I will state up front that there is no "Cinderella" ending to this chapter. What the chapter contains is insights into what makes the implementation of the Let Me Learn Process desirable, and why it is vital that secondary teachers persist in their quest to listen to the voice of the learner.

I Am a Believer

I was first introduced to the Learning Combination Inventory (LCI) during a graduate course. I was intrigued by the concept, as were other students in the class. We spent one 3-hour session taking the instrument and

AUTHOR'S NOTE: This chapter is the voice of John Evans. It presents the view of a secondary teacher as he reports how he and others struggled to introduce the Let Me Learn Process into the real-life context of secondary education where content and tests reign supreme and consideration of the student as a unique learner runs a distant second. Individuals who contributed case studies for use in this chapter include John Evans, Maureen Davis, Ellen Wightman, and Teresa Wood.

discussing our scores and what to make of their interpretations in terms of our own learning. We also discussed how this would apply in classrooms in secondary schools and what it would mean to students, teachers, and administrators.

The following year, I enrolled in a second graduate course, and again, the class was administered the LCI. Although I was impressed by the consistency of the tool, I did not expect to use the LCI for the purpose for which it was truly made: helping me become more attuned to my learning and enabling me to work with classmates in an optimum fashion. Fortunately, we not only learned about what our LCI meant, but we continued discussing its use throughout the course. In addition, our LCI scores were used to make groups of four or five students wherein we created our own schools and spent the entire semester working and learning together. For the first time in a graduate course, I experienced palpable excitement among the students.

Knowing my own LCI score made me a more effective learner. It was only natural for me to consider how I would incorporate the LCI into my classroom so that I could help my students become more effective learners.

My Voice

Several years ago, I formulated a teaching platform. Within it can be heard my voice as a learner and teacher.

> To be a teacher, we must be willing to walk a fine line between enlightenment and despair. If we can overcome the social stigma of "just being teachers," we must then confront the true challenges of the vocation we have chosen. We must be willing to accept the phenomenal responsibility of educating our future while coping with the mundane and usually trivial complications that come with being a cog operating in the monstrous bureaucratic machine we call "school."
>
> Educating young people is not simply cramming their minds with as much objective knowledge as is deemed proper by administrators. Teachers must realize that they are involved with the development of lives. Furthermore, teachers must understand that they are receiving students who are certainly not tabula rasae. Each student has been previously molded and has developed into a young person capable of making decisions. In other words, for the teacher and student alike, there is never objective knowledge without subjective knowledge. Students bring to the classroom their cultural capital, making them individuals in every aspect, including how they learn.
>
> A math teacher teaches math, a reading teacher teaches reading, and so on. Yet all teachers are teaching other values besides their spe-

cific discipline. Certainly, a math teacher and his or her students do not operate in a mathematical vacuum. The student should adequately learn the subject matter, but he or she also should learn how to abide by the social rules and expectations set up in the microcosm called the classroom, and he or she should learn to value learning for the sake of being a better person. All of what a student learns in a math class, including nonmathematical ideas, will be carried out of the classroom and eventually out of the school with that student as he or she becomes a viable citizen of the community. Because it is better to build a child than to repair an adult, teachers must understand that every aspect of the time they are with students affects the kind of person they will become.

Yet it is the authority of those who teach that is often a hindrance to those who learn. A problem exists when teachers have dug a moat around themselves and declared that because they hold the answer key, they are the "end all and be all." These teachers are not leaders of students, nor facilitators of learning; their students are completely unempowered. Effective teachers must break down these barriers; they must turn over the responsibility of learning to the students so that they can truly have ownership of their education. Teachers must reduce the risk that students feel in learning while building the trust that students need to succeed. Without being monopolizers of information, teachers must be facilitators; without being tyrants, teachers must be firm; without being friends, teachers must be approachable. Teachers need to establish classrooms that are safe, fair, and conducive places for learning to take place. In short, teachers should ask themselves, "How would we teach them if they were our own children?"

As a measure of refocusing before each new school year, I listen again to this voice. Within that voice, I hear my mission, "the teacher must understand that he is receiving a student who is certainly not a tabula rasa"; "All students bring with them to the classroom their cultural capital, making them individuals in every aspect, including how they learn"; "An effective teacher must break down these barriers; he must turn over the responsibility of learning to the students, so that they can truly have ownership of their education"; and "I will teach my students as if they were my own children."

Concurrently, when school begins, I listen to the voices of the students—their voices as learners. To hear their voices, and for them to hear mine, I use the Let Me Learn Process. It is the vehicle that promotes understanding for responsible teaching as well as responsible learning. It amplifies the voices of both the teacher and the student to work as partners toward common goals of learning, understanding, and achievement. The Let Me Learn Process encourages me not to let these voices become suppressed or drowned out by the cacophony of the loud voices of curriculum and administration, the nagging voice of complacency, or the challenging voice of adolescence.

My Let Me Learn Experience

Before I implemented Let Me Learn in my algebra classroom, I worked to put my own personal mission statement into action. Even so, I was losing my vision. I could see the blurring. I was simply teaching the way I was taught, hardly ever engaging my students. I was teaching in an "observation-safe" fashion. I was teaching and reaching only some of my students.

Having the students become aware of their Learning Combination was truly enlightening. Once students saw their LCI scores, they remarked how obvious it was to them that the scores were accurate. What I recognized was that the Let Me Learn Process gave my students and me a language by which we could discuss their learning patterns. The LCI became a vehicle for discussion, further understanding, and improvement in accomplishing the learning tasks. With the Let Me Learn Process, the muffled voice of the learner was beginning to be heard.

The first year I implemented the Let Me Learn Process, I began by selecting four students from a particular class who fit the following labels: "The Ideal Student," "The Organizer," "The Know-It-All," and "The Student Who Drives Me Nuts." My goal was to identify these students, analyze how this label was reflected in their respective LCI scores, and construct a portfolio of work for each of these students to help me filter through the static to listen and hear their voices.

The Ideal Student

I chose Maria as the "ideal student" for several reasons. First, she appeared capable and alert. Not a genius, but someone whom the other students would call "smart." Her classroom behavior was superlative, yet she was relaxed enough to still be a member of the class if it became off-track during a lecture. Her work was always neat and completed on time. She had no problems with doing any assignment given to her, from homework to a test. If she did have a problem, she never complained about it. Her grades were always in the 85% to 100% range, and she indicated that she prepared and studied for quizzes and tests. She was the type of student about whom teachers would say, "She's a pleasure to have in class."

After looking at Maria's LCI scores (Sequential, 30; Precise, 25; Technical, 30; and Confluent, 24), it became apparent to me why I had chosen her as an ideal student. A 30 in sequence showed that she was the type of person who needed to follow directions—a prerequisite for surviving high school. A 25 in precision was high enough that she was willing and able to take in all of the information given in our course. Her score of 30 in technical reasoning surprised me. I thought that she would have become irritated that we did not do more "hands-on" activities in our class. Her 24 in confluence gave her that willingness to take risks that was manifest in her regular participation in class discussions. Her scores enabled her to be a well-rounded student.

The Organizer

Lauren was the "organizer" (Sequential, 35; Precise, 22; Technical, 23; and Confluent, 14). One of the two perfect scores in the class, Lauren's 35 in sequence was an easy prediction after seeing her homework done on four or five pages, when other students did theirs on half a page. All her other work was just as thorough and neat. In class lectures, she was totally intent on soaking the lesson into herself, feeding on the step-by-step processes that I wrote out for the class on the board. However, Lauren's dilemma came when she constantly had to turn her attention from watching the proper order of solving a problem being modeled on the board to writing notes in the proper order. In fact, during a particular lesson on writing equations of lines in point-slope form from two given points, Lauren became the focus of attention in class. The problems we were doing certainly were not easy, and they involved up to 10 steps. On one problem, Lauren became lost at the third step, as evidenced by her complaints that I was "going too fast," which progressed to simply, "This is impossible!" At maybe the eighth step, a very simple process took place, and Lauren just threw up her hands in total frustration, exclaiming, "Wait, now how did you do that?" She was answered by her other 23 classmates, who had been doing a better job of keeping up and comprehending as they went along, and who were frustrated by Lauren's not recognizing the ease of the current step. Once she saw it, Lauren explained, "Okay, I see that now. It's easy. I just didn't get it because you lost me way back in the beginning." Lauren was a very good student, but she lived and died by her sequentialness.

The Know-It-All

If you were to observe Erica (Sequential, 31; Precise, 23; Technical, 25; and Confluent, 26) in several normal class situations, you would know why I chose Erica as the "know-it-all" student. She was very confident that she knew the correct answer to my question, and she was outgoing enough to let everyone know it. Her grades vacillated. In fact, on one particular test, her grade was 78%, and she was not happy with it. She was amazed that she did so poorly. "How could I have gotten all these wrong?!" she asked incredulously in front of the class.

Erica's "Use First" score of 31 in sequence, her "Use as Needed" score of 23 in precision, her 25 in technical reasoning, and her confluence "Use First" score of 26, explained why her expectation of perfection was not always realized. Obviously, Erica relied on her confluence to intuit answers rather than her precision to solve the problems. The result was a mishmash of grades and an inconsistency in performance.

The Student Who Drives Me Nuts

John (Sequential, 27; Precise, 13; Technical, 30; and Confluent, 22) drove me nuts at least once a week. The reasons ranged from ranting and raving about how easy a particular chapter was to scoring a 49% on the test the very next day, sighing as he received his test mark, "This stuff was impossible." John was only one of two sophomores repeating the class in a class of 22 freshmen. He had a tough time concentrating in class, seemingly more interested in the blandly painted cinder block walls next to him than my notes on the chalkboard. Yet out of the blue, John would often spurt out an answer that was right on the money, whereas 2 minutes later, he was on the wrong page. On a particular test where he scored 59%, he argued over the one point he needed to have a passing grade. "If I go home and fix all my mistakes, will you give me the point?" I agreed that if he fixed every single mistake to a correct answer, he would get the single point. He practically skipped out of the room with delight.

It was clear that John's score of 13 in precision was why he may have believed the material was easy, yet he had no penchant for actually gathering the facts or rules he needed to earn the grades of which he thought he was capable. His score of 27 in sequence was his lifesaver by which he could at least follow what I was showing him in class. His technical reasoning score of 30 was what I did not accommodate in class, and this did not offer him a chance to learn to use his "Use First" pattern to succeed in class. His score of 22 in confluence kept him coming back for more and did not completely discourage him to the point of shutting down to me when he did not succeed.

Teacher Voices

There are other secondary teachers with whom I teach who have also taken up the challenge of listening to the voice of the learner.

"I've Seen It Work With Mixed-Ability Classes"

Ellen (Sequential, 23; Precise, 25; Technical, 29; and Confluent, 28) is a science teacher of a mixed-ability class. Her LCI scores indicate that she uses sequence and technical reasoning "First." As a result of her new understanding of different learning combinations, Ellen began to use assignments designed to allow a wide range of approaches. She described the changes in her teaching and indicated that the easiest change she found was in giving instructions. Previously, she had always given short directions and had not been concerned. Now, with her understanding of her learning combination, she recognized that her high level of technical and lower degree of precision influenced the amount of directions and the specifics she included in them. She no longer becomes upset when students don't wish to wait for all the instructions before they start an assignment. If a student then wants to negotiate an alternative assignment on the topic, she is prepared to consider this on an individual basis. Ellen also worked to form student groups using each student's learning combination. After initial protests about not being with their friends, the students accepted that individuals with different patterns may be able to contribute their strengths to the quality of the assignment.

One assignment on the digestive system was to extend over eight periods of class time. It involved the library for research, the computer lab for illustrations, and classroom time for drafting the presentation. Ellen, aware that the class had a wide distribution of ability, initially expressed concerns over issues of control, equal levels of participation within the group, and motivation to work at the task. Ellen freely admits that her major concern was that of assessment—the bane of secondary teachers. As she says, "I like to be in control at all times and feel self-assessment will not allow me to do this." However, she did find that the discussion to set up the criteria for grading was a good lesson for both the students and herself. "Because they shared in the decision making, most tried to do exactly what was expected. I was able to factor in individual ability without explaining this to the class." Most importantly, it allowed her to continue to treat each student with respect, including those who were the more limited achievers. The success of the project has meant that she will follow the process again at another time using a similar format.

Ellen made important observations about group participation and acceptance of responsibility by individual learners (see Exhibit 7.1). She observed greater tolerance in the students for each other. She was emphatic in stating she no longer heard students using "put-downs" or insults toward one another. There appeared to be more questions asked and less embarrassment over difficulties, leading to more self-confidence and a greater level of interaction between students and the teacher. It was pleasing to see indications of more pride in their work and even spending

---

Suheyla

S = 31, P = 21, T = 17, C = 22

Highly Sequential

- Needs clear directions; often asks many questions about directions
- Likes to see models or examples
- Likes work to be neat; often recopies

Uses Precise and Confluent

- Likes work checked by teacher before graded
- Likes to be creative

Teacher's Observations of Student

- No longer embarrassed to ask questions; she knows she's not "stupid," just sequential.
- Tried to remain focused during the "Trace a Person" part of the project—wrote functions
- Organizer of group; she checked on members' progress daily

Exhibit 7.1

more time on task. One of Ellen's greatest achievements was in bringing special needs students into the classroom learning activities. "I no longer hear the excuse, 'I can't do this work; I'm P.I. (a special needs classification category—perceptually impaired).' Instead, I hear students asking, 'Who can give our group some help getting organized? We need someone highly sequential over here.'" Ellen has taken up and met the challenge of employing Let Me Learn in her secondary classroom. She has heard the voice of her students and responded.

Making a Difference and Understanding Why

Another teacher discovered the role that the LCI could play through her pursuit of total quality learning. Maureen (Sequential, 27; Precise, 29; Technical, 9; and Confluent, 26) is a history teacher. The process of change began for her when she challenged the basic premise of secondary school history classes that students must learn and remember historical facts. She began the challenge by raising two fundamental questions: Could it be that historical content (i.e., facts, dates, etc.) was secondary to

TABLE 7.1

Learning Pattern	% of Use First	% of Use as Needed	% of Avoid
Sequential processing	30	60	10
Precise processing	0	60	40
Technical processing	21	51	27
Confluent processing	28	50	22

the learning process? Was teaching the management of information (i.e., emphasizing the storing and retrieval of pertinent information) the best route for preparing students to face the next millennium? She continued her search and became very interested in the principles of Total Quality Management.

Then followed a period in which Maureen experimented with her teaching of history. She introduced shared resources, group settings, role-plays, effective questioning techniques, and issues from control theory. She decided to develop student teams: one focused on content, one on practice, and another on data. The content team decided the focus and methods for the chapter material. The practice team selected the subject and skill assignments and conducted reviews of the correct information. The data team checked student work for completion.

All students were cross-trained so that teams rotated duties with each chapter. This involvement of students in the "teaching" role dramatically improved student participation in learning. "This turnaround in my history classroom has resulted in raised test scores, diminished discipline referrals, and increased teacher enthusiasm." Once a year, students respond to an open-ended survey of their perceptions of their environment and learning process. Comments such as the following provide further and crucial testimonies regarding how their needs as learners have become integral to the environment of the classroom: "In this class I learn because I am a part of the lesson." "I have learned to lead, and I have learned to follow." "We learn the work, and we learn how to manage our learning." "This course is different because it teaches us, the students, to lead an independent classroom environment and helps us mature socially and mentally."

For Maureen, the most recent insight occurred when she administered the LCI to her students and examined their learning combinations. Administration of the LCI to 60 of her students yielded the results shown in Table 7.1.

The most notable feature of these results is the absence of precision as a "Use First" pattern. Added to that are the 40% who avoid precision. Here, then, was the recipe for disaster for students sitting in a traditional history class. Because learners who avoid precision have difficulty differentiating between important and unimportant facts, they easily become frustrated when reading fact-intensive materials. Words are not their primary means for processing the world around them. The use of brief outlines, key data, and opportunities to apply the information being learned to a real-life situation is much more productive for these learners. Multiple-choice tests and essay exams leave them frustrated and unfulfilled. For these students, a broad overview is sufficient. Anything more—such as memorization of long lists of terms, definitions, or dates—is not only painful and demeaning but also highly ineffective.

Only after administering the LCI was Maureen able to understand fully the reason for the success of her total quality learning. As she later explained, "My greatest excitement about the credibility of total quality learning results from the administration of the LCI. The instrument revealed that the only homogeneous trait among the 60 pupils in their second year of U.S. History is a will to avoid precise processing (research, answers, memorization, tests, etc.). Switching the primary focus of the class from content to process, born of my own frustration, is the key to unlocking my students' ability to learn! These data support my hypothesis that the total quality learning approach can open opportunities for successful learning in other subject areas as well."

What Maureen experienced with her students was an awakening of their interactive learning processes. Maureen's success speaks volumes for the need at any grade level to listen to the voice of the learner.

Who Changed the Most and to What Extent?

Terri (Sequential, 29; Precise, 20; Technical, 28; and Confluent, 20) used the Let Me Learn Process with her Creative Foods class. When she administered the LCI at the beginning of the course, she, like Maureen, recognized why the students had chosen her course as their elective: The majority of the students avoided or used precise processing only as needed. Her students did not enjoy accumulating facts! They wanted to express their learning through making things, applying their learning to everyday events, and coming up with their own ideas. "It was through understanding the students' combinations that I was able to make changes to the way I taught that enabled the students to enjoy my course and achieve success."

A review of the students' LCI scores also gave her another interesting insight. Eighty-three percent used sequence "First" or at the high range of "Use as Needed." This explained why they needed step-by-step instructions, examples, and enough time to finish their activity. An important part of the learning for these students was to have a beginning and an end to their learning activity. This caused many tensions as Terri also tried to comply with those regulations that demand that classes do not run over time and students must move on at the bell.

With the knowledge and understanding of the students' learning combinations, she was able to communicate to them alternative ways of doing things. "Using the inventory allowed me to get to know my students more quickly and on a more personal level." She used this information to form balanced groups—ones that matched the use of the different patterns—to provide support and direction within each group. This proved to be an asset because balanced groups were highly productive, able to solve problems, and resolve differences for themselves. It made the class a pleasure to teach.

Talking to students about their learning combinations allowed Terri to help them both with her course and with their approach to other subjects. Students who used confluence first were advised on ways to listen to directions and not just jump in in classes that required very precise details. Sequential students were helped with time management so that they could have the satisfaction of feeling that they had completed the work. Technical students were told of the need to have a folder in which to keep notes, whether they took the notes themselves or copied them from others who were more precise. Confluent students were advised to keep developing their ideas and not give up too soon so that the results of their creative ideas could be rewarded.

By listening to the voices of her students, Terri was able to form a partnership with her students. Understanding students whose patterns clashed with her patterns provided a platform of understanding that consequently resulted in less conflict or tension in the classroom. Assessment items were reviewed so that they enabled the students to demonstrate their learning in ways that matched their learning combinations. Students were able to take part in the planning of the course and in suggesting alternative ideas to be implemented within the program.

The Secondary Challenge

Being a secondary school teacher, I can testify to how easy it is to lose the vision of your purpose as a teacher. A vision of having the student at the center of the learning process can easily become a vision of completing the textbook on time. I feel the pressure to have my class be caught up with the other classes by the time of the final exam. I am under pressure to cover the prescribed curriculum. I don't have time to teach students what mathematics is used for and why what they are studying can be useful and effective in real life. A teacher's best intentions are diminished by the extreme pressure of the curriculum, tests, and district-state expectations.

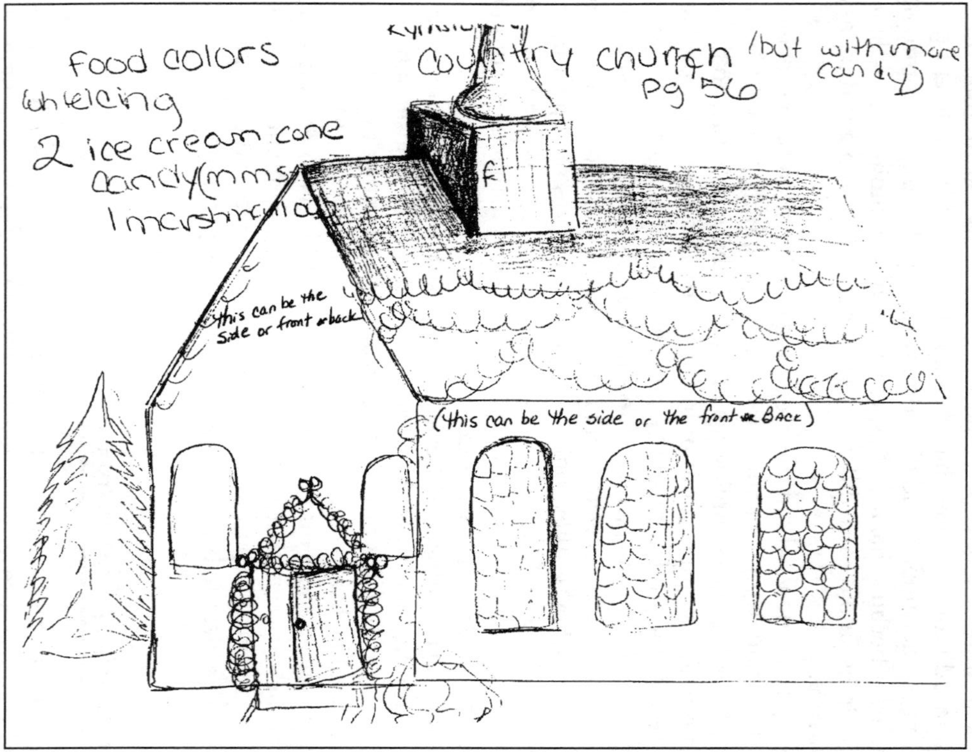
Food colors
2 ice cream cone
country church
Pg 56
(but with more candy)
this can be the side or front or back
(this can be the side or the front or BACK)

Exhibit 7.2 Student Scores: 21-17-29-29

Teacher Comments: Generates a lot of energy in the classroom; has lots of ideas; stays after and asks how to do something differently.

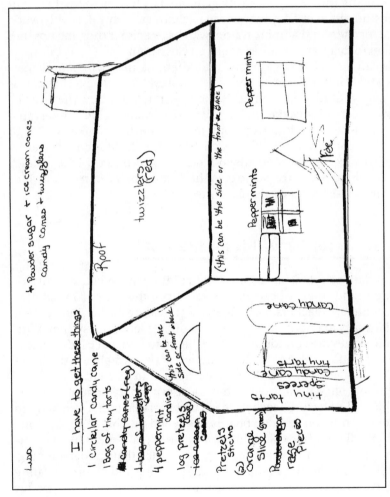

Exhibit 7.3 Student Scores: 32-25-30-21

Teacher Comments: The students were to develop their plan for the gingerbread house. Lisa was very detailed in her design and with her order list.

Although a teacher begins with a vision of having students learn about how they learn, the teacher soon succumbs to the pressure to implement the curriculum, all under the guise of getting students ready for college. The vision becomes blurred by expectations to prepare students for college, where they will have to take notes in lectures and where they will be graded on one final exam. There are other causes for this "loss of vision," ranging from the paperwork generated by having more than 100 different students every day to working in a bureaucracy filled with overwhelmed teachers and administrators who have neither the time nor the inclination to facilitate a learner-centered classroom.

How can a teacher engage students when the main concern is that Chapter 11 will not be finished and tested by next Wednesday? How can a teacher engage students when he or she does not know how they learn? How can a teacher judge the students' will to learn by looking at the tops of their heads as they furiously copy notes from the chalkboard? If a teacher does not have an overtly vested interest in the students as learners, then why expect the students to have a vested interest in learning? How can students' voices be heard over the droning of the curriculum and the churning of the school calendar conveyor belt?

Do We Have to Know This for the Test?

The secondary school is an educational culture whose god is achievement scores and upon whose altar is sacrificed the learner for subject matter. Secondary teachers see their role as providing the last inoculation against illiteracy and innumeracy before students leave the system. With that in mind, they are comfortable using the "pour it in, pack it down, and move along" industrial model whose rhythm of performance is the backbeat mantra "teach 'em and test 'em, teach 'em and test 'em."

I believe I am safe in saying that most secondary school teachers teach what will be tested. Teachers teach material that is dictated to them by curricula, proficiencies, and boards of education. Therefore, students learn what will be tested. More important, and less evident, is that students indirectly learn to value "getting by" rather than understanding. Learning becomes important not for understanding and communicating but for getting high scores on tests. Secondary schooling, when it operates in this manner, is rarely an inspirational event. In fact, perhaps "learning" is too strong a word to use to describe an event that is most often preceded by the words, "Do we have to know this for the test?"

It is this cadence of curriculum that drowns out the voice of the learner who is asking for an explanation, more time to understand, an opportunity to figure out the problem, and the attention of his or her teacher. Listening to the learner is replaced with, "Listen to me, the teacher." Listen to my directions, listen to my knowledge, listen to what you did wrong, listen to the next assignment. Within the secondary setting, the teacher's voice dominates, and the learner's voice diminishes.

To be certain, there are raised voices, under-the-breath voices, adolescent voices, but not voices connecting with learning. Yes, there are students who achieve in this environment. They are the highly precise who take notes well and the highly precise/sequential who organize and maintain the notes, memorize the information, follow the directions, and produce the work as directed.

There are also students who survive in this environment. They use their "As Needed" levels of sequence and precision to keep their frustration in check. They are not allowed significant opportunity to use their "First" learning pattern of technical reasoning or confluence. These are the students who "get by." However, the breakdown of students does not end with "achievers" and "survivors." At least one third of all high school students fail to complete secondary school, or they do so with minimal achievement scores. In a nation that prides itself on educational success, this fact should serve as an attention getter.

The Secondary School Learner's Voice Needs to Be Heard

The challenge for secondary teachers is to implement a process such as Let Me Learn that allows articulation of the curriculum material by individual learners in a variety of ways and still meets the needs of a time-pressured and test-driven curriculum. Sometimes, administrators, supervisors, and teachers are reluctant to support processes that appear directed away from the smooth flow of the tried-and-true textbook-test preparation model. However, the continued failure of this system to produce sustained outcomes is creating the need to refocus the agenda from schooling to learning.

As teachers become aware of the individual learning patterns of students, there is a stark realization that the current process is not the way in which all students are going to achieve the desired levels of performance. Some will need opportunities to express the knowledge they have acquired in different ways. I said at the beginning of this chapter that there would be no "Cinderella" ending. Yet I am more a believer than ever. The Let Me Learn Process is the sure means of making a difference with students. One thing is for certain: If we continue to ignore the voice of the learner, we will only continue to perpetuate a schooling system where large numbers of students "reach the end of their schooling with potentially low attainment levels and no enthusiasm for learning."

And This Is What They Said

A Test of Understanding

The following is a test of the reader's understanding of the points I have made in this chapter. Please complete the following test items.

True or False—Who's to Blame?

1. Secondary schooling will succeed when teachers teach better.
2. Secondary schooling will succeed when the elementary schools send us students who learn better.
3. Secondary schooling will succeed when more financial support is available for schools.
4. Secondary schooling will succeed when the number of students per teacher is reduced.
5. Secondary schooling will succeed when each classroom is linked with instructional technology.

Short Answer–Right Answer

Bonus Question: What would happen if I did listen to the secondary school learner's voice?

Write a well-composed answer. Be certain to define the terms used in each of the following statements. Be certain to follow your conscience.

1. Schooling will succeed when the voice of the learner is heard and a partnership of learning is formed between learner and teacher.
2. Schooling will succeed when knowledge is not force-fed to children, but rather when children are encouraged to construct their own ways of representing knowledge.

References and Selected Bibliography

Johnston, C. (1996). *Unlocking the will to learn.* Thousand Oaks, CA: Corwin.
OECD. (1989). *School and quality: An international report.* Paris: Author.
Santrouck, J. (1994). *Child development.* Dubuque, IA: William C. Brown.

Staff development should be innovation-related, continuous during the course of implementation, and involve a variety of formal and informal components.

Joyce, 1990, p. 4

8

Listening to Others, Hearing Ourselves: The Let Me Learn Staff Development Process

The Teachers Gather!

We teachers are constantly engaged in some form of listening. We listen for pleasure, for instructions, and for the purpose of personal and professional growth. However, most times, we really do not *listen*; we simply *hear* what is being said.

For example, we were told that the Let Me Learn Process would teach us to apply the Learning Combination Inventory (LCI) to ourselves and our students, and we would learn techniques that we could apply to our teaching to meet the needs of individual students. Our concern was that the topic of learning styles was already overdone with no lasting impact, so how could six elementary teachers in a small rural school benefit from this information? With this attitude in mind, we entered the process as individuals who were unfocused and reluctant to believe that anything of value would come from this forum.

At least we were in agreement that the focus would be on the student. We listened to what we were told would be the outcome of the Let Me Learn Process, but what we heard inside ourselves was the voice of the skeptical teacher saying, "Go through the motions, don't create any waves, get what you can out of it regardless of what the 'expert' says, and use it if and when you can in your classroom."

In our small group, the range of attitudes went from, "I'll do what you say to please you," "I know all about this, and I'll impress you with what I know," "Fine, I'm just going along with this because it fulfills a professional

---

AUTHOR'S NOTE: This chapter is the voice of Michael Buccialia, a curriculum specialist, who discusses the impact of the Let Me Learn Process on professionals as they came to grips with their own learning voices. Individuals who contributed case studies for use in this chapter are Esther Biermann, Michael Buccialia, Linda Dickinson, Sandra Dorrell, Mary Beth Foster, and Lorraine Pfeffer.

development requirement," to "I'm open to every idea and suggestion that will help my students learn," and "I'm convinced this is critical to making me a better and more effective teacher."

Our first meeting was clouded with uncertainty and mistrust because we were not listening to each other, only to our internal drivers. The above attitudes were quite evident, although there were attempts to disguise these and other feelings. However, two activities that took place in that first hour changed forever the perspective and attitude of each individual and the group as a whole, causing us to listen to each other.

The first task seemed simple and straightforward, but not necessarily easy because it was thought provoking. We were to identify and describe students in our classroom who were "the ideal student," "the one I can't reach," "the student who drives me nuts," and "the enigma." We then were to justify why we had classified these students in that way. It seemed an interesting task. In fact, it actually generated a lot of discussion because most of us could identify from our past teaching experiences the selections that others in the group made and then verify the appropriateness of the classification. This seemed to be a good mingling activity that focused our attention on the student. However, it wasn't long before we began to experience two reactions.

First, we began to see that the students we individually had selected to place in each category were students with whom each of us had had the same negative experience year after year. These were students who differed from us in how they worked in our classroom. They were unfocused, uninterested, uncooperative, uninvolved, and unwilling to buy into what we were doing.

Second, on rare occasions, we found ourselves placing a student in one of the categories totally opposite from what another member of the group would have chosen. In other words, a student who was the "ideal" student in one class was the "one I can't reach" in another. That generated very intense discussions that, for the first time, indicated we were listening to each other.

However, there was little understanding of or tolerance for how a student could be viewed so differently. We discussed the typical reasons that this may occur, such as subject content, common interests, male/female role models, and time of day. However, this did not lead to any real explanation for the differences.

The next Let Me Learn activity provided the first objective information that explained our similarities and differences in our categorizations of the students. Using the LCI, we could see for the first time who our students were as learners. When we matched our scores to those of the students we had labeled as "ideal," everything began to make sense. Student scores that were most like ours were the most accepted and understood; the opposite was true for combinations that differed from our scores. The students who were identified as "ideal" had learning combinations that matched our own! For example, teachers who used sequence and precision "First" chose students who used sequence and precision "First" as their "ideal" student. Teachers who had very high scores in confluence identified students who had identical scores. It may not be an earthshaking insight that we tend to value students who are like us, but never had we experienced a way to objectively identify and compare the learning characteristics we hold in common and then scale them for a valid comparison. This is when the project began to take on a second dimension—listening to and seeing students for who they are and ourselves for who we are as individuals and teachers.

A Time to Listen and Reflect

The second session, which focused on our selected students, provided a perspective that not only enlightened our understanding but also opened doors of opportunity for dealing with our students. We began to understand that we could change our view of students. We realized that most of the concepts, opinions, and perceptions we form of students are usually based on emotional criteria. This subjective evaluation creates incorrect, unjustified, and potentially damaging perceptions of students' motivations, desire for learning, and ability to learn. Suddenly, those square pegs did not have to have their edges rounded off to successfully fit into a round-hole world.

The voices of the students started to be heard during the next three sessions. For the first time, I understood why a student had to keep asking for directions over and over again, and why another student needed to know more information before getting started. These were classroom scenarios that would frustrate me because I don't need a lot of directions or information, and I could not understand what appeared to me to be my students' extreme need for them.

Other teachers, particularly those who were very sequential and precise, could not understand why certain students wanted to work independently of them. They couldn't understand why some students wanted to explore by trial and error their own way of doing things. What became clear through our discussions was that students and teachers do not have to be adversaries in the classroom. It isn't a challenge to our authority when students react indifferently to our instructions. It is, instead, their way of learning!

The impact of this new awareness was most evident with students who are annually and routinely identified as underachievers or problem students, or as "unmotivated and uncooperative." Their learning combinations did not fit into the neat sequential and precise orderliness of most

TABLE 8.1 Timeline of Let Me Learn Process Activities

1	2	3	4	5
Orientation	Share observation of student	Examine class profiles	Share class activities (videos)	Share second activity (videos)
Identify six learners	Learn how to interpret student LCIs	Present activities re: ILM	Discuss observation about the six focus students	Discuss what was learned about C.L. vis-à-vis videos
Take LCI for self-awareness	Look at six focus students	Discuss student responses	Discuss how to group for cooperative learning	Plan follow-up activity
Score and interpret	Discuss how to introduce LCI/ILM concepts	Examine student work product	Develop a cooperative learning activity	Discuss strategies and progress with six focus students
Review ILM and Let Me Learn Process	Make a plan	Review the Let Me Learn progression of activities	Plan a second cooperative learning activity	Rethink how to work with students
Learn how to administer LCI	Review assignment			
Review assignment				

TABLE 8.1 Continued

6	7	8	9
Midpoint assessment: What do I know about the Let Me Learn Process?	Share assessment activities (videos)	Round-robin sharing	Identify major points of learning within the Let Me Learn Process
Development of purpose; rubrics; rules of action; culminating activity; week's product	Debrief the process of assessment	Debriefing (videos)	Review student progress
Plan alternate assessment process with class (Video)	Identify the professional growth due to Let Me Learn process	Classroom visits and presentations	Establish week's product to include in portfolios of six focus students
Discuss application of assessment to six focus students	Plan showcasing of student work	Photographs and videos	Apply knowledge to real-life situation (application assessment)
	Plan for visitation	Supportive feedback	

teachers' instructional patterns. We came to the conclusion by our fourth session that these students basically don't have a chance. Submitting totally to the system is damaging to their self-worth; however, resisting the system jeopardizes their grades and creates the perception that they are not good students. This is a no-win situation for the learner and the teacher. This conflict is compounded by the fact that learners and teachers have no common language for communicating about learning.

This was an unsettling insight. No one left that session feeling very satisfied, primarily because each of us could recall how our teaching behaviors may well have contributed to not only stress, but even student failure in some instances. One teacher remarked tearfully, "I had no idea how what I was saying to him (a specific student) could have such a negative impact. If only I had understood then what I understand now."

Let's Talk

The next two sessions introduced the need for a dialogue between student and teacher on how to best evaluate what a student knows or can do. The idea of the teacher recognizing and understanding how a student learns, the student coming to the realization of who he or she is as a learner, and the two then being able to communicate is the foundation to building a real learning partnership. An example of a revelation that occurred during the sessions profoundly illustrates the need to understand individual learning combinations based on the LCI and not on our subjective evaluation of surface indicators.

The situation involved a student who is identified as being academically gifted, which she easily demonstrated, even to the point of dominating the class. However, in other classes, she would become so methodical that she often did not complete work in class or at home. In those classes, before getting started, she would have to organize everything on her desk, read and number her paper, and arrange everything just right. Then, after this 6- to 8-minute ordeal, she would start the assignment, only to be confused and have to ask a number of questions. This is the child who, not 10 minutes earlier, was a management problem when trying to control her enthusiasm to participate. Normally, we would have assumed she did not like the subject content or teaching methods being used. Both teacher and parents took the traditional route of cajoling, threatening, and punishing her based on what we interpreted to be a display of insubordination.

It was not until her present teacher administered the LCI that there was an accurate accounting of who she was as a learner. Her scores in precision and sequence were just as high as her scores in confluence. She could, and would, choose the combination that best suited whatever the situation might dictate for her success. The subjects where her preciseness and sequentialness dominated caused her to take more time and proceed methodically and precisely. For example, in math, she did not trust her confluent pattern to carry her, whereas in language arts, she would spout answers and constantly debate. In writing class, she returned to using her precision, to the point of frustrating her teacher to the maximum. What an easier year it would have been for all of us if we had known her learning combination and supported her learning pattern when she was a student in our classes!

Assessment: Is It a Fair and Equitable Judgment?

One issue that we each struggled with was assessment of student learning outcomes. Here, we found that subtle biases abounded, creating within the teacher the need to carefully think through the nature and fairness of the evaluation procedures being used. A sixth-grade teacher explained a situation she had experienced.

> *I gave my students a test that involved developing answers to several open-ended questions. When I got their tests back, some felt that they told me everything they needed to tell me in a sentence, while others took several sentences to explain. That did not surprise me at all. However, the kids who I thought gave the best answers were the ones who answered the way I would have answered the questions. Insight—it is not easy to determine the level of understanding or comprehension when we base our judgment solely on the length of a written response!*

Another member related a personal experience when her husband and she took a college course together. "I took voluminous notes, and he took next to nothing. He knew much more than I and could apply the information. However, on the exam, I wrote paragraphs, and he wrote a couple of sentences. If you compare the two, we both said the same thing. However, I got an A and he got a C."

The facilitator of our training clarified both situations with a personal experience.

> *I did a workshop where a very highly touted professional in math and science from ASCD looked at the briefest of exam responses and explained, "I know what that is. It is a button, and if I want to know more, I just click on the button and an entire file menu drops down." The highly technical learner who either avoids or uses precision "As Needed" is simply saying, "Here's the pertinent information. If you want to know more, then just ask me."*

Information, words, amount of words—suddenly, we found ourselves confronted with our learning processes being the guiding factor for establishing how to assess learning. We had faced the enemy, and it was us! We spent a number of hours developing, rehearsing, and reflecting upon the authentic assessments we could develop with our students as a result of that eye-opening session on learning and assessment!

Let's Listen

We as teachers must not just view our students differently; we must view ourselves differently as well. We must be able to listen and understand what students are telling us. One of the group members stated it best.

> *I can now see how children, especially those who are different than I am, approach learning. So now that I recognize some of their values and some of what they would prefer to do, I think I can be more understanding and more flexible as a teacher. I've also allowed them to see myself as a learner, and we can help each other and give each other strategies.*

Nearing the last session, we shared details of the progress within our classrooms. It was clearly evident that the next level of change that had occurred was our taking time to listen to our students. Other staff members were now hearing positive feedback about the effects of the Let Me Learn Process, particularly the willingness of students to interact and cooperate with one another. The Let Me Learn Process now took on a new dimension.

As one of the group members described:

> *My class has had a reputation for not being able to get along, so group work has always been a challenging process. They now see value in themselves. They value each other and what each can bring to the group. Now, after they meet as a group, they can turn to the highly technical learner and say "Well, how would you do this?" whereas before that learner would have been totally ignored or tuned out.*

For the first time, there was a common language to describe the learning process that was distinct enough to be easily interpreted.

Another teacher used a videotape of one of her activities to vividly portray to her students what was happening and how people can be taken for granted. She explained,

> *My students who use precision "First" are very precise, and sometimes they won't listen to other students, especially the students who use tech-*

nical reasoning "First" and precision "As Needed." I had one project in which one of my highly technical and moderately precise kids went off and read a book by himself because no one was listening to him. When I showed the tape to the group, they had no clue that by not listening, they had totally excluded him. From that point on, there has been an obvious change and a sincere effort to include him and all students in the projects. Most importantly, those who are reaching out feel better about themselves when they accept the responsibility for the impact they can have.

What we recognized was that students who were a part of the Let Me Learn Process now possessed a way to communicate about their learning, so not only did they understand themselves better, but they also learned from others who were different. What we were now experiencing in our classrooms were students who understood and appreciated each others' differences.

Communication Builds Strong Supportive Relationships

During the final session, we focused on how the Let Me Learn Process had affected each of us. We identified a new sense of interdependence within the group. We discovered the same positive attitude growing within our classrooms. We realized that this was the result of old walls and defenses breaking down and new relationships being built upon communication. For the first time, there was a way to communicate and develop an understanding of why we do what we do, and why others do what they do. Toleration was on the increase. We were all touched when one of the teachers in the group brought into the meeting a student-drawn picture that depicted an improvement in this student's interaction with his classmates since participating in Let Me Learn.

The increased tolerance for different ways of learning allowed for greater acceptance by classmates. The more accepting students became of each other, the more open they were to discussing with one another who they were as learners, thus reinforcing a bond of trust.

The impact of this was evident in the fifth-grade classroom. This was the class described earlier with a reputation for poor personal relationships. Their teacher describes their behavior toward a student whom they had outright rejected in the past. "The students are much more understanding and tolerant even to a point of encouraging him. They included him and even asked his advice. It used to be that he was very suspicious of anyone who said anything nice to him. He can now accept that better."

Exhibit 8.1

Exhibit 8.2

The students are also recognizing and accepting the differences of other students, particularly those who do not fit in the typical school profile. "Students deal with others with much more toleration, especially those who are very confluent and in the past were thought of as being weird. Now they recognize they are not; they are just exhibiting their learning patterns."

Dynamics: More Than
Just Listening—Communicating

A whole new world opened for the student and teacher as a result of the Let Me Learn Process. Teachers could now not only predict how students would react to learning situations and experiences, but more importantly, they communicated with their students and their students with them. The student became more comfortable working within specific guidelines that had meaning and value for him or her. This cooperative effort resulted in greater understanding and built a more supportive relationship between teacher and student.

Changes in Students

Our group now began to understand the implications of the Let Me Learn Process for our students. This occurred through two dramatic examples—both occurring in the sixth grade. The teacher related the impact on the student who was very capable, yet not directed or focused. He was on medication for ADHD, but there were other drivers that prevented him from producing. Often, it was his perception of himself as a learner. She stated in a review of his year,

> *As Matt grew to understand himself as a learner, two things happened. First, Matt chose to fill a role as the technical man on any team. He took great pleasure in finding divergent solutions to problems, but always wanted to stop there, leaving everything else to the rest of the group. As time progressed, the group would not permit him this luxury. Others in the group, who understood the need to become balanced in all ways, required Matt to do his part. At year's end, I could see a much higher level of organization and follow-through in Matt's work than I would have believed possible. His final research project was complete and well-executed, and the organization and content were there as well.*

Real Learning Outcomes

We have only scratched the surface of student learning—the potential of teachers to empower student learning and the implications of how this will have an impact on their families. A fifth-grade teacher summed up the value of the process. Using her highly sequential list-making behaviors, she wrote:

Unlocking the Will to Learn Culminating Activity

Please bring four portfolios; one for each of the students you chose to focus on. In each folder, place the following:

1. Your initial description of the student, that is, the card that includes the category under which you placed the student and the description you initially wrote

2. A copy of the student's LCI

3. An example of how the student initially demonstrated his or her understanding of his or her Learning Combination

4. Any work product that you feel demonstrates the student's Learning Combination

5. Any work product that you feel demonstrates the student's intentional use of his or her Learning Combination, as in cooperative learning groups or at times of assessment

6. Any anecdotes that you recorded concerning your interaction with the student or the student's interaction with others

7. Your current description of the student (insights, progress made to use his or her Learning Combination more effectively; sense of self as a learner; parents' feedback, etc.)

8. A statement of demarcation concerning the issue of change: Who changed? When? To what extent? With what outcome?

Be prepared to present the two most complete portfolios representing the most vivid examples of growth, development, and change. Be prepared to answer the question:

In handing over this child to next year's teacher, what would you say to prepare the teacher to receive and work with this student? What would you tell the student to be prepared to do when he or she begins the school year with a new teacher?

Exhibit 8.3

I now

- *Understand different learning combinations better*
- *Present information and assess pupils in more flexible ways*
- *Am aware that some students may need more assistance in working within traditional educational settings*
- *Understand myself better as a learner, teacher, and parent*

I think my students as learners have

- *Grown to appreciate others' strengths as learners*
- *Learned to be their own advocates (to negotiate points to better demonstrate their mastering of material)*
- *Taken on more responsibility for their own learning*

Changes in Group Interaction

The same teacher describes the results of a cooperative learning activity in which the students were grouped together to form balanced groups using their learning patterns. She observed the following through the course of the activity:

- Students who were working in mixed groups interacted naturally with lots of constructive discussion.
- Students stayed on task.
- Students moved in and out of groups, seeking support.
- Students felt free at times to separate from the group and work totally alone.
- Students located classmates who could provide strength in certain patterns they needed; willing help was given.

The greatest impression I have of the change in the students was that they were consistently on task and reaffirming to one another. The class manageability was incredible. They began work right away; they organized themselves and were able to progress independently. There was more attention paid to presenting a thoroughly complete project than I had seen in the past, and the motivation appeared to come from within the group.

Student letters to the district superintendent were very descriptive in the analysis of themselves and the validation the inventory gave them— that they were okay as learners. One sixth grader wrote, "I don't like taking notes. I don't like reading out of books, but that's all right. I like to listen to people and feel that's all right for me. I'm very technical and sequential. I avoid precision and confluence. I'm not the smartest kid in sixth grade, but I'm trying. I don't like to work with other kids, but that's okay. I like to do things myself, to make things. I always worked by myself, and I am happy about that."

Another student writes, "My most commonly used combination is sequential. I like answering questions and reading for information. I am very organized. I do everything step-by-step. I think this program [Let Me Learn] is helping me learn more and more every day. I think everyone is learning more, sequential or not."

A third student writes, "I need clear directions and I need to be organized. I love being taught in a way where the teacher gives you information packets with instructions. If I can't have information that way, I like to work with partners, to help each other and do the things that each of us do best."

These communications clearly demonstrate the project's value and impact on students. They effectively could communicate their understanding of learning patterns and how that understanding dramatically changed each one's perception of themselves as a learner and as a person. They were empowered by this knowledge.

A teacher in the project commented,

Having analyzed, recognized, organized, and realized our learning combinations with my class this year, I am astonished by what we are now able to do. Each student (including me) is now responsible to understand how we approach a learning task, distinct from every individual. We are capable of determining which learning process fits best for each task, and we seek to draw on our natural inclinations if they fit. We also recognize that if we need to use a process that is not a strong one for us, we can look to classmates to model for us how we can do what we need to do. This process has the potential to open my students as well as me to greater learning now and in the future.

Changes in Teachers

This mutually shared reaction and interaction is the catalyst for real change in classroom instruction. Although more responsibility is placed on the student, the teacher's role becomes much more sophisticated and reaches beyond the content. The remarks of the skeptic in the group follow:

I got involved with this project not because I thought it had any value or that I was ever going to change the way I taught. Especially to incorporate a type of approach that just seemed to make excuses for students plus lessen the expectations and standards for their learning. I anticipated that eventually I would be expected to do this training, so I wanted to find out all I could about it in order to defend my resistance to incorporating it into my classroom. However, I never found what I was looking for. Rather, I became empowered as a teacher, able to change my instructional strategies to meet the needs of my students and to see them for who they are as learners and people.

I totally support the project and have entered into discussions with those who have been closed-minded about it. I know the value of the inventory and its ability to assess how students learn. I have experienced a change in attitude in my classroom, validating both the students and me. I am very high in sequence and precision; my scores in technical reasoning and confluence were both 14. Most of my instruction in the past has been very traditional.

As a result of going through the Let Me Learn Process, I have taken a second look as to how I assess student learning. For example, I gave the students a list of things they could do to demonstrate their understanding of the literature they had read. They wanted a free period to work on it, and although I was still uncomfortable with that idea, I gave them the opportunity. We designed a number of ways for evaluating all the presentations. In the end, the presentations were outstanding. They were more detailed than I would have ever expected, and they were much harder on themselves than I would ever have been. They will be allowed to surprise me again!

Celebrating and Sharing Achievement

Excitement about the Let Me Learn Process did not stay in the school building. The students soon began using the vernacular of the process to describe their learning experience to the parents. Soon, parents became involved. Their initial reaction, after taking the LCI, was, "Hey, this really is me." "That's exactly how I learn." "Now I know why he (my child) is the way he is." "This is going to make our family life a lot easier, because it now makes sense why we all do things differently, and we will be more tolerant of each other."

The most important result of encouraging parent involvement and sharing this information with them was the common statement: "I really want to help my child with his/her homework and be an active part of his/her education, but it has always been a major conflict. We just seem to end up frustrating each other, not completing anything without a great deal of difficulty. In other things we get along fine, but we just don't seem to communicate when it comes to learning."

One parent illustrated it most vividly:

Trying to help my child at home with homework is like two trains on separate tracks. We start out together very slowly, headed in the same direction and with every intent to complete our journey. But what started out in a parallel relationship gets disrupted very quickly. We go at different speeds, start to crisscross each other's path, and many times end up on a collision course, only to be sidetracked. Most of the time, we finally get there, but what an ordeal! The worst of it is we'll start it all over again the next night. With this new knowledge and understanding that we are different and why, I'll be able to make adjustments and be more supportive of my child. We will head in the same direction, be tolerant of one another, and interact with one another in a constructive way.

Everyone Is Empowered to Become a Better and Continuous Learner

The ongoing result of the Let Me Learn Process is that students', teachers', and parents' perspectives of themselves are changed forever. Students are no longer bound to the traditional boundaries of the classroom. They are no longer limited by narrow requirements and expectations. They are empowered to learn to the fullest extent of their potential and ability through processes that are most effective and efficient for them. Teachers will never "tune out" students again. They will never see or expect to teach in a single dimension to a single audience of students. They will see and hear each student for who he or she is—a person and a learner.

By reaching that goal, the teacher will never have to lower expectations or goals for subject content, students' interpersonal relationships, or classroom management. Parents have a more complete understanding of themselves and their children. Their time and energy can now be focused on what support and encouragement their child needs rather than disarming their child's built-up frustration. Most importantly, everyone has learned to listen to one another, to value the communication, and to work together to create the optimum learning experience for the student.

Never did any of us anticipate the outcome. Never could we have foreseen the impact that understanding learning combinations could have on the students, the staff, and the community. Never would we have believed that just by focusing on the students' learning processes, we could hear their true voices and understand who they were as learners.

And This Is What They Said

It is very important to each of us that we be able to demonstrate what we know and to have our work fairly and equitably judged. The end result is a dramatic change in attitude toward learning and a rekindling of learning enthusiasm.

Reference

Joyce, B. (1990). *Changing school culture through staff development.* Alexandria, VA: Association for Supervision and Curriculum Development.

Further Reading

Fullan, M. (1990). *Changing school culture through staff development.* Alexandria, VA: Association for Supervision and Curriculum Development.

Johnston, C. (1994). *Empowering the organization through professional talk.* Dubuque, IA: Kendall/Hunt.

Leithwood, K. (1990). *Changing school culture through staff development.* Alexandria, VA: Association for Supervision and Curriculum Development.

Seashore, C., Seashore, E., & Weinberg, G. (1991). *What did you say? The art of giving and receiving feedback.* Columbia, MD: Bingham House Books.

Sparks, D., & Hirsh, S. (1997). Staff development, innovation and instructional development. In *A new vision for staff development.* Alexandria, VA: Association for Supervision and Curriculum Development.

There are many important relationships within a school: child-child, teacher-teacher, child-teacher, parent-teacher, parent-principal, parent-parent. I am convinced that none of these relationships has greater effect on the quality of life under the roof of the school house than the relationship between teacher and principal.

Barth (1990, p. 19)

9

Applying the Let Me Learn Process: An Administrator's Experience

Changing Perspective

Like most educators, I embarked on my teaching career with the intention of making a difference. I felt successful as a teacher, my evaluations were positive, I was affirmed by my peers, and the majority of my students were achieving good grades and successfully performing the tasks I had given them. However, I continued to wrestle with many questions, such as, "What happens to the students' desire to learn?" "Why is it that despite my efforts, students are not more active participants in their learning?" and "Why am I working so hard to reach my students?" I spent many hours throughout my career reflecting on my teaching and how I could grow professionally. It was through this process of reflection that I realized that the responsibility for learning could not be the teacher's alone; it also had to be the students'. Learning had to be a true partnership in order for it to be successful.

I feel very fortunate because it was at the time when I was struggling with questions and self-doubt that I became acquainted with the Let Me Learn Process and the Learning Combination Inventory (LCI). My experience with the Let Me Learn Process provided me with valuable insight and changed my perceptions of how learning manifests itself. Through use of the Let Me Learn concepts, I began to understand the learning process within myself (Sequential, 34; Precise, 28; Technical, 10; and Confluent, 19) and started to understand student learning. Using the Let Me Learn Process in the classroom during my last 2 years of teaching, I was able to give the learner a voice. I listened to their voices and developed instructional strategies that were successful and effective for each of them. The learning partnership that I was able to develop with my students

AUTHOR'S NOTE: This chapter is the voice of Judith McLaughlin, a school administrative leader, who, as she conferenced, coached, disciplined, and supervised, using the Let Me Learn Process to guide her in her interactions with teachers, parents, and learners.

187

was incredibly successful and rewarding for both student and teacher. For the first time, I felt that I was truly making a difference in their lives because I understood each learner.

It was at this point in my life that I became a school administrator and continued my mission of making a difference in children's lives. As happens many times when I begin a new challenge, I wrestled with many questions and felt the discomfort that comes with change. I wasn't sure how the concepts of the Let Me Learn Process would work within the context of administration. What happened was that the process became my frame of reference for administration. Let Me Learn changed who I am as an educator and how I view learning.

Understanding my own learning combination gave me valuable insight into myself and how I handle situations. It has given me insights into all areas of professional and personal relationships. The benefits in my professional life as a school administrator are experienced every school day as I communicate and interact with students, staff, parents, and the larger learning community.

A Broader Focus

I find that the job of a school administrator is much more than management. When you look at the Latin origin of *administer* (*ad ministrare,* meaning "to stand by the side of, to counsel, support and provide care for," which is really what school administrators do), the job seems even more challenging. My personal goal in my position is to create a shared learning and working environment. However, creating an environment where everyone works together as educational partners is easier said than done.

In an effort to achieve my goals, I continually keep in mind that the learners, the teachers, the parents, and the larger learning community are the people to whom I "minister" on a daily basis. The Let Me Learn Process has helped me communicate and administer by giving me a way of listening to the learner and providing me with a message to communicate. My administration has now evolved into decision making that is based upon my listening to and understanding the learner and the teacher.

As stated previously, the Let Me Learn Process has provided a frame of reference for educational administration, communication, and decision making so that when I am faced with typical, daily school issues, I now think:

- Will the outcome of my decision enhance the child's learning process?
- Will the outcome of my decision support the teacher in facilitating a healthy learning environment?

- Will the outcome of my decision enable parents to be stronger partners with their child, their child's teacher, and the school community in general?
- Will the outcome of this decision create a partnership among learners, teachers, parents, and even other schools within the larger learning community?

These questions serve as a guide to direct decision making and communication. Positive answers provide the means by which to develop shared partnerships and a nurturing learning environment.

When teachers and students form partnerships based upon knowledge of each other's learning patterns, they are able to create an atmosphere in which they have an opportunity to formulate specific techniques or strategies for using their learning patterns effectively. So too, when administrators and teachers form partnerships based on knowledge of each others' learning patterns, the outcomes are positive. All learners regardless of age, gender, ethnicity, cognitive aptitude, or physical capability seek to have their learning process understood, respected, and nurtured. Basically, all learners want to be stood by, counseled, supported, and provided care—administered to—in order to feel affirmed! Administrators have a tough job! The development of students, teachers, parents, and the community as educational partners is a big part of it.

Staff Interaction

By administering the LCI to the staff, I began to know the learning patterns of various individuals and was able to predict the approaches they would use to accomplish tasks. This information has been extremely beneficial to me. This knowledge has raised my level of awareness and has helped me understand the dynamics of the faculty. It has opened up insights into my relationships. I think carefully about how I will present tasks to faculty. I take into consideration who I am dealing with and how he or she functions. Working within their comfort level is a quick way to accomplish the tasks. I am sure to give step-by-step directions to those who need them and supply leeway for those who want to create or work independently. An example is how I work with the guidance counselor (Sequential, 22; Precise, 25; Technical, 23; and Confluent, 30). She works well if given an objective and simple framework. I realized this when I gave her the task of coming up with a way to manage third graders who had become somewhat unruly at lunch. She came to me very uncomfortable, telling me that she needed more details and an objective upon which to focus. I stated an objective, gave a detailed summary of what I wanted, and, like magic, she was off and running. She returned with an excellent plan that included charts, contracts, and so on regarding cafeteria etiquette. A plan that, believe it or not, turned our rude cafeteria goers into mannerly diners (most of the time)! I recognized that the counselor's level of confluence was such that she was not comfortable in using the ideas of others, and her level of precision did not allow her to begin without numerous details, but once given the framework and the details, she would use her learning combination to develop a very creative approach to improving lunchroom behavior based on my idea.

I also have figured out that the first-grade teachers want to be given a brief idea of what is expected. They like to take a project and run. When given specific directions, they are not as creative as they can be, producing a very basic product. With this in mind, I often give them free rein of assignments, and this has yielded wonderful results. This information about the staff is so beneficial. It saves time and effort on my part and fosters positive working relationships among the faculty.

Observation/Evaluation

Having an understanding of learning changes what I see in classrooms and allows me to assist teachers in developing successful strategies. It is great to be able to use this learning process to improve instruction. Last year, I had the opportunity to observe a veteran kindergarten teacher—the kind of teacher you look forward to visiting because her class is so exciting and active. She certainly lived up to her reputation in this lesson. The teacher was teaching about the needs of animals, and she was using cooperative learning strategies. The teacher instructed the students, explained their task, and grouped the students, giving each child a different-colored hat to indicate the role that that child was to perform in the group. The roles were the typical recorder, presenter, facilitator, and materials person.

The lesson was going well, and the groups were working well together for the most part; however, I could not help but notice that a little boy was having a conflict with his group. This fellow wanted to switch hats with his classmate. He clearly was not comfortable being the recorder. He did not want to write anything down. I smiled to myself, thinking that he must avoid precision! At the kindergarten level, this was not a problem that interfered with the lesson, but not understanding a student's patterns can create a problem in the upper grades. I used this observation to begin a discussion about student learning. As it turns out, the student's LCI scores confirmed my suspicion (Sequential, 24; Precise, 9; Technical, 26; and Confluent, 31). Having this information to offer the teacher was an asset to the postobservation conferencing process.

An example of a lesson where the children were not successful in working cooperatively occurred when I was observing a fifth-grade class.

The teacher was using cooperative learning with a science lesson. She grouped the students and assigned roles. Some groups were able to figure out how to work cooperatively, but not all of them. Two groups were in complete turmoil. Group members were obviously not in their comfort zone. They fought and ended up not completing the task. What they did accomplish and present was not to the satisfaction of their group. In writing the observation, I took into consideration that this teacher did not have the insight into the learning process and was not able to group the students effectively for success.

The postobservation conference became a starting point for me to assist this teacher in understanding learning. The point is that when the teacher understands the Let Me Learn Process, she can group children and talk to them about cooperative learning and how they function in a group. My knowledge of Let Me Learn helped me coach, not criticize, the teacher. Understanding how learning occurs and using the Let Me Learn Process has enabled me to speak a common language from which learning can be discussed and a shared learning environment can be created.

Student Interaction

One of the perks of being an administrator is that I am responsible for student management, maintaining order before and after school. My knowledge of the Let Me Learn Process has changed my discipline techniques. For example, I was extremely frustrated with a child (Sequential, 24; Precise, 26; Technical, 35; and Confluent, 17) who was chronically late. I called his mother several times, and she assured me that her son was leaving home at the correct time and that he was walking to school when she left for work. I spoke with the child numerous times, and he promised he would try to walk faster. Needless to say, the problem worsened day by day.

Frustrated, I set out on foot to find him on a day he was 5 minutes late. Lo and behold, I walked less than one block to find him. He was standing in the middle of a construction site conversing with the workmen on how the backhoe operated. I called him to me, and he explained, "I needed to stop today. Every day I walk by and wonder but can't figure out what is going on. They are finishing up. It might be my last chance." Was I annoyed? You bet, but I walked away from the situation understanding more about the child than ever. He was naturally drawn to the operations, as indicated by his high technical score, and interested in all the details, as evidenced by his high level of precision. After he knew how they worked, he walked by briskly and arrived at school on time. I spoke with the boy to discuss his future plans for arriving to school on time, and he quickly responded, "That won't be a problem. I know what's going on, and I don't have to stop anymore." Several weeks later, he announced the completion of the housing project. He has been on time ever since, but I can only wonder what will happen when the road construction begins!

Another administrative duty includes being in charge of the fifth-grade safety patrols. Their job is to "patrol" the children on the buses. When they witness unsafe bus behavior, they are to file a written report regarding behavior incidents to me and be a part of the "investigation process" and the resolution. I found myself working well with the majority of the children but having a bit of trouble relating to a few of the patrols. The few I had trouble with would report in a way that seemed haphazard and incomplete. I called one of the patrols into my office, (Sequential, 22; Precise, 16; Technical, 28; and Confluent, 21) to inquire why she was not taking her job seriously. She was puzzled. I explained that her reports lacked detail, and it appeared that she was in a rush when she wrote them. Her reply was enlightening. "I know the details and all the circumstances. You just have to ask me. I didn't think it was necessary to do all that writing." Indeed, she did know the details, and I learned a lesson. Had I known that she avoids precision and uses technical reasoning first, I would have understood her way of reporting. From that point on, I made an effort to know each patrol and his or her learning patterns. Their reports became telltale signs of how to work successfully with them.

Connecting With Learners

The Let Me Learn Process has provided a means to communicate with students about their learning in a way they understand. Most of the time, the children who get my attention are those involved in a discipline incident or those who are a parental/teacher concern. Rarely do I have the luxury of spending 15 to 20 minutes one-on-one with a student to discuss his or her learning, but I finally have made the time.

It was in working with our Student Success Program, commonly referred to as a Pupil Assistance Committee (an intervention strategy used to assist at-risk students that provides a support system for the children experiencing learning difficulties), that I saw where I could begin to incorporate my knowledge of the Let Me Learn Process. I volunteered to administer the LCI to the children referred to the committee. This was beneficial for me. It allowed me to become connected with the children and their learning.

I administered the instrument to a third-grade student on a Friday afternoon, and we spent several minutes afterwards discussing how he learns. I sent him back to class, and Monday morning, he showed up in the office and asked to see me. He came into my office asking, "Are we going to have more meetings to talk about me and my learning?" I explained that we would not, but that I would keep up with him because I see him from time to time. As you can imagine, every time I see him, I ask how he is doing, and he offers an in-depth report of his learning and classroom activities! Another student, a fifth grader, sat and discussed her learning with me after taking the LCI. When I made several statements about how she is most comfortable learning, she asked, "How do you know all about me?" Once again, a connection was made, and my new friend reports about her learning every chance she gets.

Learning about the students in our school is a never-ending endeavor. However, it is one that is very rewarding. The students with whom I interact regarding their learning view me as more than an authority figure—they consider me a partner in their education. This in itself makes the effort and time well worth it.

Parent Interaction

Teachers who understand learning are equipped with a valuable parent communication tool (a sample letter to parents explaining the LCI is shown in Exhibit 9.1). As a teacher, I used the parent component of the LCI to explain a child's learning to his or her parents. I sat with each parent at conference time and discussed the learning characteristics of their son or daughter. This information served as a catalyst for talking about how the child learned, and it gave the parents strategies to use at home. Parents who came to me frustrated because they did not understand their child and why he or she did not learn the way they did or the way other siblings did were comforted when I could supply reasonable answers. I continue to use information about how we learn in conferences with teachers.

As I previously stated, I currently serve as an active participant in our district's Pupil Assistance Committee/Student Success Program. This intervention committee, designed to assist the students who are experiencing difficulties in the classroom, consists of various staff members. Through this committee, we ask parents to attend a meeting in which their child's progress is discussed. What a difference in the outcome of the meeting when we can offer insight into their child and explain how he or she learns! Each child referred to this committee is given the LCI, and the results are analyzed with the classroom teacher. The committee then brainstorms strategies that can be used in the classroom and at home to assist the child in achieving success. Parents who attend this meeting leave having a better understanding of their child. They leave having some viable answers and successful strategies to use at home. Parents have commented that they were grateful to learn about their child's learning.

One parent in particular came to an intervention meeting in tears. She broke down, saying how she could not understand how she could

Dear parent,

Your child, _____, has taken the Learning Combination Inventory. This inventory is designed to help students understand their unique approach to learning. It is important to stress to your child that these results are not to be viewed like tests. There is no right or wrong—no good or bad. No combination is better than another. The four parts of the combination all work together to form your child's learning combination.

To understand each of the four parts of the learning combination, read the next page of descriptions. Notice the sentences that your child circled. Talk together about these. Listen to your child's explanation. Encourage your child to use his or her unique combination when in school and at home.

Exhibit 9.1

have a "dumb" child. Through her tears, she claimed that every night she engaged in a screaming match as the child tried to complete homework. We explained to her how her child learned and discussed why he was not succeeding in the classroom. Through this discussion, the mother realized that her child was not "dumb"; he just was not succeeding because he did not naturally learn the way the teacher was teaching. She was assured that we would give the teacher and her son the strategies needed to achieve success. She agreed to use the same strategies at home. She left comforted and later sent a note to the coordinator that for the first time, she felt like a partner with the school. I cannot explain in words how gratifying it is to be an administrator in a school where parents feel they are partners!

Spreading the Word

As principals and administrators, we are in positions to create positive change in our working environments. We can make a difference within our schools. Therefore, it is up to us to spread the word about understanding and reaching the learner. I truly believe that it is extremely important for all of the entities of the school to be included in a Let Me Learn staff development initiative. This step is critical if they are to understand the Let Me Learn Process. Most importantly, be sure to include all members of the school intervention teams because they operate diagnostically; they evaluate and prescribe based on information from the classroom teacher. I participate in the referral process that a student faces when he or she begins to experience difficulty in the classroom. I have witnessed how the intervention teams (Child Study Team, Pupil Assistance Committees, Student Success, etc.) benefit when they know how a particular child learns. Having a sense of how a student learns most comfortably will frequently provide insight into why that student is experiencing certain problems in a particular classroom or in completing specific kinds of tasks. The information regarding student learning serves as a guide in formulating and recommending strategies to help the student achieve success.

Pupil Assistance/Special Education

I know firsthand the importance of understanding the learner, and I witness this every time a student referral is completed. I recently was involved in the referral of a third-grade student (the student referred to in the Parent Interaction Section) who was performing poorly in the classroom. Those involved during the Student Success Meeting were considering retention or classification. After interviewing the child and administering the LCI, I found him to be extremely technical (Sequential, 26; Precise, 22; Technical, 33; and Confluent, 23), so technical that he asked if he could submit a plan for installing burglar alarms for the hall lockers! I soon discovered that this child was capable of achieving; he was just not comfortable or successful with the pencil-and-paper assignments he was given. From this observation, a learning strategy action plan was developed. The classroom teacher worked with the child and began discussing with him how he learned best. The child completed the third grade, not with flying colors, but he did earn the privilege of going to the fourth grade.

I continued my learning partnership with this student as he entered fourth grade, and, needless to say, this fellow is busy learning, learning, learning! He continues to despise long writing assignments and relishes hands-on projects that he has to figure out. However, as he becomes more aware of how he learns best, he is achieving much more success. In fact, this once-struggling student searches the Internet for projects where he can invent something. He currently is working on the Craftsman Young Inventors Awards Program. The objective is to invent and build a tool or to modify an existing tool. He also is encountering a much better relationship with his mother (the crying parent). This example clearly demonstrates the development of a positive partnership between the school and family. Understanding the learning process provided the insight needed to encourage support and acceptance of a child and his or her learning.

The process of classifying students into special education when they have not been able to be assisted through pupil assistance programs is currently the cause of many concerns. Many school districts are losing special education funding and are requesting fewer student referrals. This leaves teachers and administrators in a quandary and the student at a loss. However, I have found that the LCI and the Let Me Learn Process can serve as a bridge connecting special education and regular education. In fact, after becoming familiar with the Let Me Learn Process, I have begun to rethink the process of classification, labeling, and remediation of students. I am of the belief that all students share common concerns and common learning needs and are capable of developing a learning partnership with their teachers.

For the school administrator, the universality and use of the LCI has far-reaching implications. One is the potential for partnerships that can be developed between special education and regular education teachers.

In a world where the two are distinct entities, the idea that application of the LCI and the Let Me Learn Process works across the board is thrilling. In fact, the insights into students whom we have been classifying suggest that we may have acted in haste. Clearly, the LCI needs to be used before we would even consider classifying a student. An example I experienced was seeing a videotape of a seventh grader (special education student) involved with three other seventh graders, interacting and participating positively and successfully. The staff was flabbergasted because we thought that the student couldn't be successful in a regular education class. Ever since second grade, when she was classified, teachers had been worried about her success. After taking the LCI and being involved in a class where the teacher was trained in Let Me Learn, the student explained, on tape, to other students how she uses her sequencing and precision when she goes home and makes fill-in-the-blank tests to practice for tests she takes in school. She actually went home and worked using her learning processes to teach herself, and we thought she simply could not learn.

This student was in a special education class learning in a hands-on, concrete manner, when what she needed was more of a precise, sequential approach. Obviously, this child had several learning difficulties, but she has learned how to make her learning work at its peak performance by consciously using her learning patterns.

Another example is that of a young man, classified as learning disabled since second grade and held back a grade. This student stated, "Once other people understood how I learned, they began to like my ideas." Now his regular education teacher has him in her class all day. He is in the process of being declassified because he is working, producing, and succeeding!

What was discovered was that these students' learning patterns are masked by their learning disabilities. For example, if a student needs precision, that is, facts, information, specifics, and an exact vocabulary, but does not have the means by which to retain that information because of attention deficit or loss of short-term memory, the student is perceived by the teacher as unable to "handle" information and therefore is not exposed to detailed information. However, the student, as a learner, needs specifics. The student, as a result of this lack of match between what he or she needs and what he or she is receiving, becomes frustrated and gives up on himself or herself and learning in general. What a tragic result!

After working with the Let Me Learn Process, I learned a hard lesson. I had to admit that I had played a part in classifying students, declaring that they were learning disabled when they may have been successful within the regular education or an inclusion classroom. If only I had understood their needs and how they learned! Using the LCI with all students allows the teacher to understand the learner as a learner and to develop a working partnership. If we listen to the voice of the learner, we find that all children have a learning combination. Our job is to help them understand it and use it to its fullest potential. My experiences have made me realize, ever so clearly, the importance of Let Me Learn within the classroom and the school. Our ultimate responsibility is to the learner; classification of the students as learning disabled can and should be a last resort.

Staff Development

I recently participated in a week-long Let Me Learn course where the school principal and the curriculum director were active participants in the school's staff development effort. This situation is definitely an example of shared partnership. I was so impressed with the unity exhibited by this staff that I inquired about why the district chose to explore the Let Me Learn Process. The administrator, in this case the principal, explained that several teachers attended a Let Me Learn awareness workshop and relayed information to her regarding how Let Me Learn could help in their school. She in turn investigated the concept and felt it was a great idea. Thus, the shared decision to embark on a staff development project emerged.

Together, the principal and teachers developed action plans based on the Let Me Learn Process and are implementing their plans throughout the school year. The principal sees many areas where Let Me Learn can help the school in its effort to improve. Her overall plan is to focus on reducing the special education population and the number of referrals given to the Child Study Teams. The staff feels that if they can understand the learning process, and thus understand their learners, they can reach them in ways that they were not able to before.

This partnership approach is so worthwhile. The teachers expressed that they feel that the principal is with them, working as a partner to

Lesson Plan for Let Me Learn Faculty Meeting

Objectives:

1. Participants will gain new understandings about themselves as learners through discussing their unique learning combination and the characteristics of the four learning schemas.
2. The teachers will realize the importance of patterns within a pattern by circling their preferences for learning on the four parts of the worksheet (My Learning Combination) and then compare and contrast their responses with other colleagues of a similar combination.
3. Working in a cooperative group of mixed learning combinations, the teachers will brainstorm classroom accommodations for an assigned pattern. There will be four groups, each with a different pattern assigned.
4. Working with the same group, they will design accommodations for students who avoid a certain assigned pattern.

Materials:

Teachers' completed LCIs, My Learning Combination Worksheets, Learning Combination Characteristics Chart, chart paper

Activities/Procedures:

1. As the teachers enter the faculty meeting, they will pick up their completed and scored LCIs and sit in groups. The characteristics of each learning schema will be discussed. They will be asked to compare and contrast patterns to see if anyone in their group has the same pattern and the same numbers.
2. The teachers will then circle the learning characteristics that best describe them on the My Learning Combination Worksheet. They will discuss with a partner how their patterns-within-a-pattern may differ.
3. The large group will then regroup into four groups with mixed LCI characteristics. Their task is to brainstorm accommodations that would be appropriate for this child. The ideas will be listed on chart paper to share with the group.
4. An "I avoid" pattern will then be assigned to each group. Again, they will brainstorm classroom accommodations to assist this student in being successful with these types of tasks. The ideas will be charted to share with the group.
5. Each group will choose a spokesperson to share their ideas with the whole group.

Evaluation:

Completed group charts of appropriate classroom accommodations will be shared with the group. Individual My Learning Combination Worksheets will also be completed.

Exhibit 9.2

understand the learning process, and will be active in extending that understanding to the other entities in the school. They also know that when they experiment with various instructional strategies and means of assessment, the principal will understand, and their evaluations, observations, and so on will be based upon common ground. This has made a positive difference in the attitudes of the teachers. The teachers in this situation share a commitment with their principal to improve their classrooms and their school.

One teacher explained, "It is easy to commit when you know you are in it together." Each person in this staff development is a part of the Let Me Learn Process; they work together to understand learning, develop effective instructional strategies that meet the needs of the individual learners, and implement meaningful assessment practices. They made a connection and are on a continuous journey, as teacher and learner. On their way, they plan to reach each student while developing successful learning partnerships within their school.

Committing to Partnerships

For educational partnerships to develop, the learning community within the school must work together to create positive, enduring changes. These changes begin by listening to the voice of every learner in the community! A commitment to the Let Me Learn Process provides the means to do this. Everyone must understand and implement the process for learners to be understood and achieve success. It is extremely important for administrators to be active participants in the staff development endeavors. A partnership cannot be formed if one of the partners is absent.

I truly know firsthand the time constraints and pressures on building principals; however, I have found that the concepts of Let Me Learn have made my job and life easier. It is suggested that administrators who support and implement the Let Me Learn Process handle it as a comprehensive staff development project and not through a hit and run, fragmented approach. A difference can be made in children's lives if we, the administrators, continue to support teachers and their efforts with students as they reach each one by listening to his or her voice.

Every learner has a voice. By listening to them and understanding who they are, relationships become stronger and partnerships form over time. The most challenging issue facing educators as we move into the 21st century remains reaching the learner so that student growth and achievement are maximized. The message of Let Me Learn holds great potential for accomplishing this.

A Personal Reflection

The concepts of Let Me Learn have raised my level of understanding of others and have opened up insights into my relationships with them, some of which are difficult. This knowledge has been most beneficial as I continue to strive to create partnerships, professionally and personally. The self-knowledge gained by understanding how I learn has enabled me to perform in ways that are most beneficial. For example, writing this chapter was not an easy endeavor for me, but understanding who I am as a learner made the task a bit easier. Being sequential, I struggled when I could not see an organized method to my writing, but I agonized and strategized to reach the end. Some questioned why I would take on this task along with all of my other obligations. The answer was simple: Like every other learner, I wanted my voice to be heard.

And This Is What They Said

Learning about the students in our school is a never-ending endeavor. However, it is one that is very rewarding. The students with whom I interact regarding their learning view me as more than an authority figure; they consider me a partner in their education. This in itself makes the effort and time well worth it.

References and Selected Bibliography

Barth, R. (1991). *Improving schools from within.* San Francisco: Jossey-Bass.

Johnston, C. (1997). *Unlocking the will to learn: Teachers and students as partners.* Paper presented to the annual conference of the British Educational Research Association, York, England.

Further Reading

Covey, S. R. (1991). *Principle-centered leadership.* New York: Summit.

Manno, B., Finn, C., Bierlein, L., & Vanourek, G. (1998). How charter schools are different: Lessons and implications from a national study. *Phi Delta Kappan, 79,* 488-498.

Marshall, S. (1995). The vision, meaning, and language of educational transformation. *School Administrator, 52*(1), 8-15.

Sergiovanni, T. J. (1992). *Moral leadership.* San Francisco: Jossey-Bass.

Part III

Pumping Up
the Volume

We began this book by emphasizing the importance of listening. We conclude by emphasizing the importance of action. Good intentions will not make a difference with our learners; focused action based upon the commitment to make a difference will! This final section examines the commitment needed to implement the Let Me Learn Process within a classroom, a building, or an entire school district.

Every child is a perfect work
waiting to be revealed.

Ruth Silverberg, on Michelangelo,
Personal communication,
February 17, 1998

10

Making the Commitment to Listen to the Voice: The Measure of It All

A Measure of Understanding

After completing the previous nine chapters, the reader knows that learning is a wonderfully complex event. Learning is the result of more than the firing of neurons, the cascading of multiple intelligences, or the capriciousness of personality. Like all of our world, it is much more ordered in its chaos and much more dynamic than a single categorization. Learning consists of more than brain science alone, multiple intelligences alone, or learning styles alone.

What We Know

We know that the complexity of a learning event occurs as a result of the interaction of our cognitive processing, conative performance, and affective development. We know that the interaction of four basic patterns domiciled within the hard-wired patterns of the brain form our distinct learning combination. We know that unlocking that combination is possible. What we don't know is what our response to all this "knowing" will be. For after all of the reading is done and all of the information is digested, the real measure of our understanding of learning will be seen in what we choose to do. Will we continue to devote 12 years to reshaping our students' learning mechanisms into school learning, or will we accept and appreciate each learner's way of learning and devote time to developing the learner's potential?

A Measure of Resolve

After several hundred pages, the issue comes down to the reader's resolve to act. The questions are straightforward: "What are we prepared to do

AUTHOR'S NOTE: Individuals who contributed case studies for use in this chapter are Jo Anne Glass, Ann Hostetter, Leslie Kohler, and Susan Stone.

once we have heard the voice of the learner?" "What will we do with our newfound understanding of learning?" If we are not prepared to facilitate learning, then it is better to operate with the policy: Don't ask, don't tell. We should not seek to find out who the learner is if we intend to take no action. Make no mistake! To discover the essence of the learner is to assume responsibility for encouraging, engaging, and empowering the learner.

Understanding what makes learning work for a child is not frivolous knowledge. This is sensitive information that explains the intricacies and complexities of the soul of the learner. Such knowledge does not leave us in the same state as it found us. It will haunt us and challenge us to grow and change. As one teacher related,

> *I participated in the project [Let Me Learn] because I can't fight against something I don't know about. So I decided, "I'll go into the program and learn about it and find the reasons why I don't want to do it, and then say it's no good." So I came in, and I was changed. The change wasn't sudden, but I have changed. I'm much more open to my students' suggestions now. I am more willing to let them do different types of things. Given the fact that things may not be as I planned, my acceptance of this really shows how I have changed.*

Learning about learning is not for the fainthearted educator who does not possess the resolve to make a difference. Learning about learning will not allow a teacher, a school leader, or an educator simply to maintain the status quo of the classroom—a status quo where

- "Creative, highly social people are shut up in a room all day long studying algebra, English, physical science, and world history." (Hartman, 1993, p. 406)
- "Teachers teach wonderful subject matter in orderly, disciplined classrooms to students who are not learning." (Clinchy, 1998, p. 48)
- "Young people are underwhelmed by their school experience of relentless memorization which leaves them exhausted of ideas." (MacBeath, 1997, p. 13)
- The most common phrase spoken at parent-teacher conferences is, "bright, but not working up to capacity."
- "Ability groups, grade retention, college pressures, working alone, denial of strengths and focus on weaknesses lead students to depression, dropping out, drugs, jail, and suicide." (Barth, 1991, p. 126)

Although many voices, including those of academics, politicians, and parents, call for relief on behalf of the learner, as practitioners, we are in a position to do something about it.

The Measure of Our Resolve

The measure of our resolve to act rests upon our ability and willingness to confront four significant "Yes, . . . but" questions. These questions consist of standardized tests, state-mandated curricula, teacher willingness to change, and parents' expectations.

Living With the Reality of Standardized Tests

This section of the text will not enter into a debate on the saliency or legitimacy of standardized tests because the jury is in on this question, and the verdict reads, "In our frenetic pursuit of testing, there is a real danger that we leave the immeasurable gifts and competence of our children behind." However, we would be foolish to ignore the degree to which our national educational-political climate has been seduced to use cost-efficient, easily administered paper-and-pencil tests as a means of quantifying student achievement. Therefore, there is no doubt that we need to be prepared to answer, "Yes, I agree that the best means of ascertaining what the student knows is through authentic assessments such as portfolios, but we are still required by the state to administer standardized, nationally normed tests. So what do we do when the students' scores on standardized achievement tests aren't what they should be? How do we explain this to parents? How do we defend the time we spend on helping learners understand their learning combinations? Wouldn't our time be better spent on skills and drills that directly apply to the things about which our children will be tested?"

The answer to this "Yes . . . , but" dilemma is straightforward. Students who know who they are as learners and are engaged in learning for understanding can apply this knowledge about themselves as learners to any testing situation. Whether standardized tests of multiple choice, true-and-false, fill-in-the-blank, and short answer, it simply makes sense that learners who understand their learning patterns will be better able to read and comprehend what is being asked of them on these tests.

For example, most standardized tests are developed with items that become progressively more difficult. For the learner who understands and uses the sequential pattern "First" or "As Needed," this progression of difficulty in the test items is understandable. Thus, when they see the first 3 of 10 items under the math section, they can attack these with confidence knowing that these are very "doable." That same student can proceed through the remaining items with the knowledge that the next four will be of middle-level difficulty, and the last three will be the most challenging. Such understanding of the progression of items can allow the test-taker to anticipate the increase in challenge by recalling how the math instruction linked the use of one insight to the next type of problem to be solved. Students do not need to be overwhelmed and defeated when they come upon the challenging phase of each section. They can talk themselves through it without carrying a sense of hopelessness into the next section of the test. They are, instead, prepared to begin each section with a strong level of assurance and a spirit of resiliency.

Remember, the affective portion of our interactive patterns is what feeds our "I can do" sense of learning. It is imperative that if we are to keep students from giving up and shutting down during standardized testing, we need to help them understand the structure of the subsections and the opportunities for success that lie within each of them. This is particularly true for the learner who "Avoids" sequence or uses sequence at the lower end of the "As Needed" range. For these students, the test is a jumble of hit-and-miss questions that appear to be randomly confronting them.

A student can learn to demystify such tests if and when he or she is given the opportunity to recognize not only the intentional structuring of the test but also the nature of the individual who wrote the item. For example, the precise answer being sought on a multiple-choice question can be easily misperceived by a student who uses confluence "First." In such a case, the student reads the item written by someone who uses precision "First" and who is expecting one exact answer. The confluent test-taker spins the intent of the question into an array of interesting, albeit misguided, interpretations. As someone who uses confluence "First" and precision in the "As Needed" mid-range, I can testify to how I respond to multiple-choice questions. I read the multiple-choice stem and immediately begin to apply my own unique interpretation to what is being asked. By the time I look at my choices, I have completely missed the point of the question and convince myself that none of the choices is correct. I allow my confluence to overpower my precision and head me in the wrong direction.

How many times have I heard learners who use confluence "First" and precision "As Needed" lament, "I couldn't find an answer that made sense." Then, as we talked about what the question was specifically asking, I would hear, "Oh, that's all they were looking for? I thought they wanted . . . ," and the learner begins to explain some very interesting probes that were far beyond the depth and complexity of the answer being sought. "If they'd only let me use my own way of explaining, I could have shown them what I know. It sure would have been more interesting than the choices they gave me to choose from!"

For students who "Avoid" precision, multiple-choice items with embedded discrete choices play havoc with their learning combination, leaving them feeling defeated and frustrated. We have had success in coaching these learners. By pairing them with a learner who uses precision "First," these students have learned how to identify key names, dates, terms, and so on that are guaranteed to be a part of the test questions.

Then, working with the learner's combination of patterns, we have strategized how to "crack" the system of multiple levels of choices within each question stem. In one instance, we helped a student strengthen the content of essay responses, which had previously been critiqued as wonderfully interesting and fluid but without sufficient specifics. By encouraging the student to revisit the names, dates, and terms from the multiple-choice items, the student was able to reference these specifics in the essay response.

When the student called in tears to say she had passed a Western Civilization exam with a "B," it was evident that this learner had conquered that form of testing for the first time, and she was now prepared to do it again and again. No more questions of, "How is it possible that I attend every class, keep a well-organized notebook, read the text, and stay up all night studying and memorizing and still do not succeed?" The learner had succeeded because for the first time, the preparation for the paper-and-pencil assessment matched both the task and the learner.

The converse frustration can be true for those who use precision and sequence "First" and find themselves out of time or unsuccessful when writing essay responses. As a learner who uses confluence "First," I always received high scores on holistically scored essays that required risk taking. On the other hand, my classmates who were more precise or more sequential struggled to finish within the time allotted and labored to stay well within the confines of what they thought were the rules and parameters of the topic.

The answer to "Yes to authentic assessments, but we still must perform well on standardized tests" is to use our knowledge of our learning patterns to demystify standardized tests. In doing this, we can build the confidence needed to attack these "necessary evils" and prevent a loss of self-esteem. Just as we have learned to unlock our learning combinations, we can unlock the test items and overcome the fear induced by their cold, unbending demand for one right answer.

We have seen how students can become proficient in surmising the test writer's Learning Combination Inventory (LCI) scores and using them to intuit what skill or information the test writer wants the student to demonstrate and understand. Students can then develop strategies that unravel the "system" and lower the level of their test anxiety. Strategies include examining the correct answers and why they were correct; listening to how different learners figured out the correct answer; and attending to the feelings of students as they express their concerns or fears of completing certain portions of standardized tests (open-ended questions, essays, etc.).

Schools who have used these approaches have experienced dramatic improvement of childrens' scores on standardized tests. This is more than "test-besting" or "teaching to the test." This involves helping students use who they are as learners to conquer their fears of the mysterious entity that enters their classrooms once a year, taking out-of-context snapshots of their performance on a feat heretofore not a part of their lives, their classrooms, or their learning mechanisms. Instead of providing excuses for not succeeding on standardized tests, the Let Me Learn Process actually empowers students to overcome this hurdle, which has been used inappropriately to define and label their status as learners.

Living With the Reality of Mandated Curricula

The next "Yes, . . . but" question involves the unrelenting cadence of mandated curricula. Here, there is ready agreement that much of the lock-step, production-line curriculum that is being generated by federal and state agencies does not allow teachers the opportunity to work with students as learners. Instead, it requires that every minute of every school day be devoted to the imparting of subject matter. Yes, this is not healthy. Yes, this is not realistic. Yes, this flies in the face of all we know about how children learn, but . . . the pressure is on. We must cover this material by the end of the marking period, the end of the year, the end of . . . end of . . . end of, regardless of its lack of positive effect upon the student-learner.

To this "Yes, . . . but," the response is simple and direct. Understanding one's learning process actually expedites learning rather than creating an added burden. Listen to the voices of teachers who held those concerns and who later found their concerns unsubstantiated:

> The Let Me Learn Process is not another stand-alone piece of the curriculum—not just one more thing to do. It is the substance of what our learning is made of—it doesn't take time away from learning. It only enhances what we are doing.

> I watched as we became more understanding of what the LCI scores told us about ourselves as students, and as we played with that knowledge in the various projects attempted. Before long, that knowledge seeped into everything we did in the classroom: daily lessons, assignments, reports, even homework.

> I was reluctant to become involved in the Let Me Learn Process because I looked at it as something extra to do. I love teaching, and I enjoy the work. Just don't give me extra things. I don't want to do it. I like what I am doing. Then I became involved with Let Me Learn and saw that it only made my work easier because the students took hold of this information about themselves and made it work for them.

The Let Me Learn Process does not add another layer of anything to the curriculum. Instead, it infuses the curriculum-learning process by empowering students and teachers alike to teach and learn more effectively.

Living With the Reality of the Threat That Change Brings

Change, even when done for the right reasons, can still be threatening. "Yes, I would like to understand my students better. Yes, I would like to see them thrive and enjoy learning. Yes, I am committed to learning and growing, but the actual change in how I do things, the actual coming to grips with my own biases about learning, the actual time required for reflection and mental regrouping—well, I am not certain I am ready for that."

The Let Me Learn staff development process has a significant effect upon those who participate in it. Their change in perceptions on teaching and learning are deep and far-reaching. A conversation with a teacher who participated in the staff development process helps explain the change that occurred:

> *I am feeling excited and encouraged. The Let Me Learn Process is beginning to come together for me and my children. I know we still have a long way to go. I do believe, however, that these children will leave third grade with a better understanding of themselves as learners. Perhaps this year, they really will feel that love of learning I speak about each year at Back to School Night.*
>
> *When we finished reading the novel, The Haunting of Grade Three, I decided to attempt our first group project, putting students into groups, careful to mix and balance the students' learning combinations. The classroom came alive. Almost everyone became an active participant. As I stood and watched, I, too, had a new outlook on learning.*
>
> *My sequential, precise teaching self was not totally comfortable with the lack of organization in the room. Yet I wasn't totally frazzled. Although I hadn't given anyone step-by-step directions, lots of good things were happening. I could see that this group of students will need lots of learning opportunities like this, and I know I am able to adapt my learning combination to meet their needs.*

Another teacher explained change in this way:

> *The staff development focused on children's learning. But in doing so, change occurred in our teaching. Now I understand that changes in neither teaching nor learning will be effective or long term unless we look at these as parallel activities. By working in this way, no one felt threatened or coerced to change. We felt invited and supported in our change.*

Clearly, one strength of the Let Me Learn Process is the building of a community of professionals who are undergoing change simultaneously.

As one teacher remarked, "All six of us came in with different levels of tolerance of our students' ways of learning, and we've all grown to be more tolerant." This degree of professional growth can be attributed to the removal of what has typically been described as the "state of semi-isolation" that exists among the professional staff within our schools. The Let Me Learn intensive schedule helped the participants make connections with each other and optimize their relationship. Yes, change occurred, and yes, it was a challenge, but not one teacher of those who engaged in this process has ever expressed a desire to return to the state of teaching at which he or she began the process of change!

Living With the Reality
of Parents' Expectations

Joshua's teacher and mother were frustrated because he was not performing to his fullest potential. Despite all of their efforts, Joshua was failing every test. To prepare for a test, both the teacher and parents would drill and drill and drill. The goal was to have him learn the necessary information and succeed. After months of futile effort, Joshua's parents, suspecting he had a learning disability, asked that Joshua be evaluated by the Child Study Team. The evaluation ruled out any learning impairment. Now, both parents and teachers were truly stumped.

The school year concluded as it had begun, with Joshua failing. At the beginning of his seventh-grade year, Joshua's teacher administered the LCI to him. A conference was set up between his teachers and his parents. It was determined that Joshua was a highly technical and sequential processor who avoided precise information. Now all involved knew where to begin.

Once Joshua understood himself and that the way he was learning was not wrong, he was more at ease with his learning process. He relaxed and began to take the time necessary to study "his way" instead of the way others told him was correct. He had to go through his own process of sequencing the information and putting it into a format that made sense to him. In the beginning, he would ask for help to identify what, precisely, he needed to know or understand. He then worked diligently to figure out how to make himself succeed using his patterns in his way. As a result, Joshua completed the seventh grade as an achieving student no longer frustrated by failure. Now he would tell you that he actually enjoys learning activities.

Yes, parents have expectations for their children, and yes, they are concerned whenever something new is introduced into the school program, but in the case of Let Me Learn, parents have openly embraced its content and outcome because the process has helped them better understand their own children. As one parent-teacher stated,

I have always felt that people—both children and adults—do learn differently. It has always been common sense to me that some teachers just don't "click" with some students, and some parents just can't seem to relate to their own children. Now I recognize that what may well be the source of conflict is a misunderstanding of each other's learning patterns. Understanding the LCI has helped me to understand the combinations of my own children and my students.

Another parent wrote the following to a teacher who was using the Let Me Learn Process:

As you know, my daughter is a highly confluent learner. The training you and she received afforded her the opportunity to explore several assignments from her unique perspective. You have been her best means of support in dealing with learning situations which are not easily handled by confluent learners. She has always recognized a difference between herself and the rest of her class and felt badly. This year, she was shown to be different, but because of your support, she thinks this is pretty neat. Thank you for all you have done with my daughter this year.

Finally, a letter received by a teacher who was using Let Me Learn read,

From our son's lips to you, he said you made the difference for him. It was sweet the way he said it: "She helped me believe I could do it." Well, you inspired success in our son, and we are extremely grateful for the difference you have made.

A Measure of Commitment

This deep change occurs only when those involved in it are highly committed to increasing their awareness of how we learn, act upon their new knowledge, and take the time to review with their peers their newly attained insights. Most importantly, change occurs and "Yes, . . . but" questions are most effectively dealt with in a nonthreatening atmosphere wherein participants can revisit their thoughts and actions without concern for criticism or correction.

Thus, I conclude this text with a set of challenges:

- I challenge the reader to listen to the voices of learners and teachers who have explored the Let Me Learn Process.

- I challenge the reader to investigate the difference that this knowledge and understanding can make for the learner, the teacher, and the parent.
- I challenge the reader to remain uncomfortable, unsatisfied, and unwilling to accept the status quo of our current classroom settings.
- Most of all, I challenge the reader to continue to explore what goes on in the human mind when learning is occurring, for only then will we continue to hear the very important voices of our learners.

The future of all learners depends on your willingness to listen with your heart, your mind, and your very soul to the message that each learner's voice conveys: "Let Me Learn!"

And This Is What They Said

The revelations in this book are like knowing the truth. Once you know it, you can never deny it in your heart.

R. GRANDIN
Personal communication,
February 27, 1998

References and Selected Bibliography

Barth, R. (1991). *Improving schools from within.* San Francisco: Jossey-Bass.

Brooks, J., & Brooks, M. (1993). *The case for constructivist classrooms.* Alexandria, VA: Association for Supervision and Curriculum Development.

Caine, R., & Caine, G. (1997). *Education on the edge of possibility.* Arlington, VA: Association for Supervision and Curriculum Development.

Clinchy, E. (1998, February 4). Different drummers. *Education Week, 17,* 48-49.

Hartman, E. (1993). A change of course. *Phi Delta Kappan, 75,* 405-406.

Kiesler, C. (1998). Affirmative action and the SAT. *Education Week, 17*(24), 42, 60.

MacBeath, J. (1997). Learning to be intelligent. *Education Journal, 14,* 13.

Walton, S., & Taylor, K. (1998). How did you know the answer was boxcar? *Educational Leadership, 54*(4), 38-40.

Wiggins, G. (1993). Assessment: Authenticity, context, and validity. *Phi Delta Kappan, 75,* 200-214.

Afterword

We began reading this book as two school administrators/doctoral students searching for understanding about what happens in the minds of the children, teachers, and scholars with whom we spend our lives. We emerged as empowered professionals, parents, spouses, and, most importantly, learners ourselves.

Thirty-three combined years of teaching and administering and 35 years of parenting had convinced us that there was something fundamentally wrong with the way our learning had been approached and the way we were expected to approach our students and professional staffs. We had seen students who were different, and we tried to "fix" them. As students, our teachers had tried to fix our lack of organization, our difficulty in completing projects, and our tendency to have our "heads in the clouds." (We are S25, P20, T10, C22 and S17, P17, T31, and C27, respectively.) The problem was that we had only one kind of tool that would lead to success in school, so we tried to turn our students and ourselves into sequential/precise learners. If the only tool you have is a hammer, everything starts to look like a nail.

When the fixes didn't work, we determined that they and we were "unfixable." There were times that we were able to hear and respond to the learners' voices, and this gave us the moments that kept us in our classrooms. But there were too many who got away from us without ever knowing the joy of connecting to the world we had tried to give to them.

Christine Johnston has given us the interpreter for the learner's voice so that it will never again be an accident when we hear and understand. Today is different.

As teachers, we can hear, respect, and involve every learner of every age.

As administrators, we can empower teachers with a tool to help them answer the question, "What can I do with this child?"

As administrators, we can communicate to all parents that their children can and do learn; they do not need to be fixed.

As students/scholars, we can find others with complementary learning combinations with whom we can collaborate and produce something that is far superior to anything we could create alone.

As a husband and a wife, we can hear our spouses when they tell us the way they come to understand our thoughts and hopes and dreams.

As parents, we can exorcise the ghosts of the children we didn't understand and tried so desperately to mold into "good students."

The ideas in this book have the power to redeem. The joy of growing and learning without limitations is available to every learner, whether he or she is a first grader, a graduate student, or a professional in the field. Christine Johnston has given all of us who care about children and learning and schools an easily understood approach and accompanying tools that can give voice to every person's cry of "Let me learn!"

We believe in this book.

JOSEPH RELLA
RUTH SILVERBERG

Index

CORWIN
PRESS

The Corwin Press logo—a raven striding across an open book—represents the happy union of courage and learning. We are a professional-level publisher of books and journals for K–12 educators, and we are committed to creating and providing resources that embody these qualities. Corwin's motto is "Success for All Learners."